ROBIN
VOLUME 1 REBORN

ROBIN

VOLUME 1 **REBORN**

CHUCK DIXON
ALAN GRANT
writers

NORM BREYFOGLE
TOM LYLE
pencillers

DICK GIORDANO
STEVE MITCHELL
BOB SMITH
inkers

ANDRIENNE ROY
colorist

TODD KLEIN
TIM HARKINS
letterers

BRIAN BOLLAND
cover art

BATMAN created by Bob Kane

ROBIN VOLUME 1: REBORN

DC Comics, 4000 Warner Blvd., Burbank, CA 91522
A Warner Bros. Entertainment Company.
Printed by RR Donnelley, Salem, VA, USA. 10/2/15. First printing.
ISBN: 978-1-4012-5857-3.

Library of Congress Cataloging-in-Publication Data

Dixon, Chuck, 1954-
Robin. Volume 1, Reborn / Chuck Dixon, Rom Lyle.
pages cm
ISBN 978-1-4012-5857-3 (paperback)
1. Graphic novels. I. Lyle, Rom, illustrator. II. Title. III. Title: Reborn.
PN6728.R576D56 2015
741.5'973—dc23
2015031544

BATMAN IN
Detective
COMICS
APPROVED BY THE COMICS CODE AUTHORITY
618
LATE
JUL 90
US $1.00
CAN $1.25
UK 50p
DRAKE
PLANE
LOST
GRANT
BREYFOGLE
GIORDANO

Cover art by Norm Breyfogle

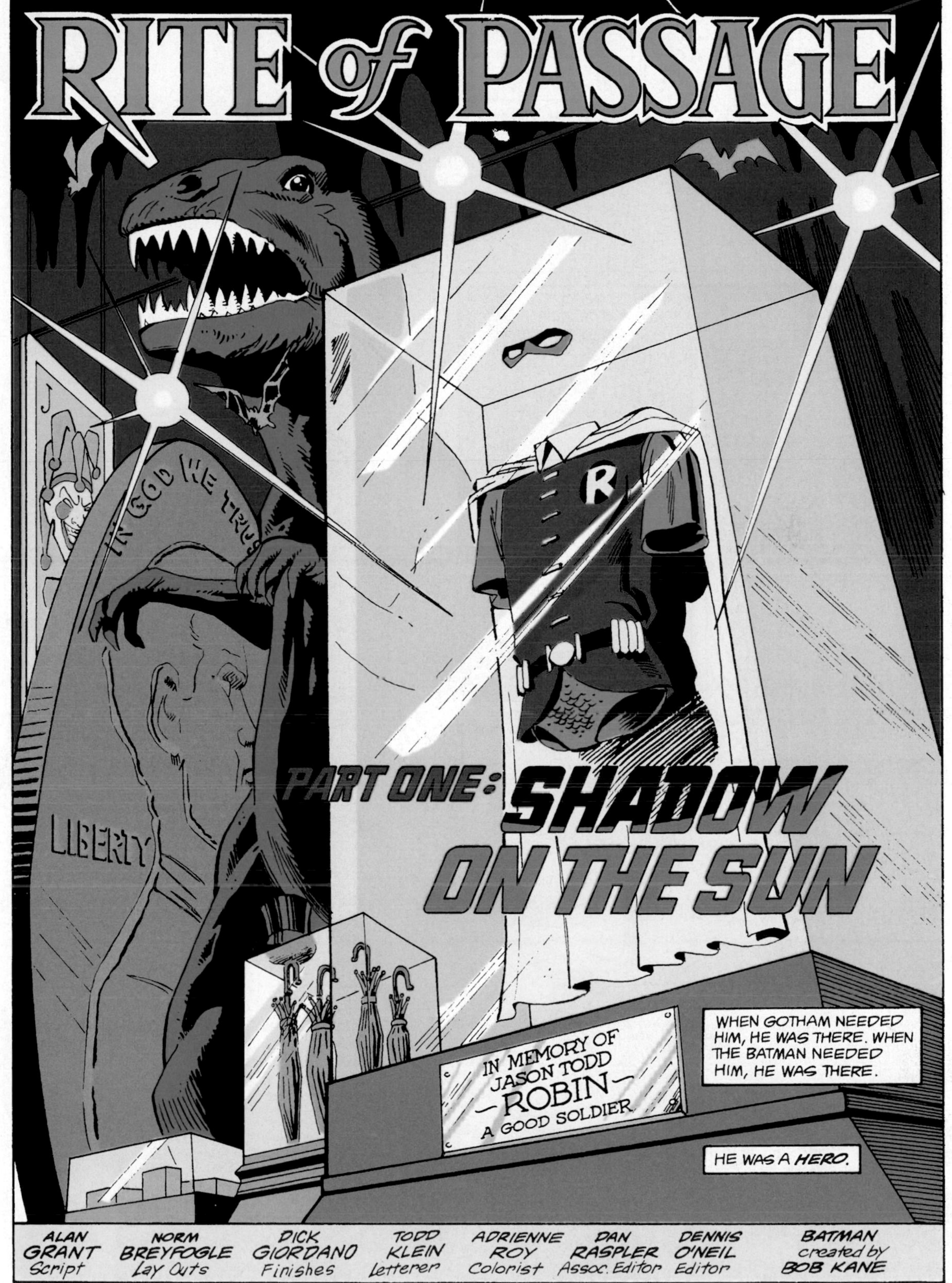
RITE of PASSAGE
PART ONE: SHADOW ON THE SUN
IN GOD WE TRUST
LIBERTY
IN MEMORY OF JASON TODD —ROBIN— A GOOD SOLDIER
WHEN GOTHAM NEEDED HIM, HE WAS THERE. WHEN THE BATMAN NEEDED HIM, HE WAS THERE.
HE WAS A HERO.
ALAN GRANT Script
NORM BREYFOGLE Lay Outs
DICK GIORDANO Finishes
TODD KLEIN Letterer
ADRIENNE ROY Colorist
DAN RASPLER Assoc. Editor
DENNIS O'NEIL Editor
BATMAN created by BOB KANE

BUT HE WAS NOTHING SPECIAL, REALLY. JUST A BOY, WHO WAS TAUGHT--TRAINED--BROUGHT TO HIS FULL POTENTIAL BY SOMEONE WHO KNEW HOW.
JUST A BOY...
...LIKE ME.
I CAN DO IT. I KNOW I CAN.
ONE DAY I'LL BE AS GOOD AS JASON. ONE DAY I'LL WEAR THE SUIT.
ONE DAY I'LL BE A HERO.
2

BLEEE BLEE BLEE BLEE BLEE BLEE

YOU'VE FOUND HIM?
BLEE BLEE
NOT YET, I'M AFRAID.
BLEE BLEE
IT ONLY MEANS THE COMPUTER HAS COME ACROSS A SERIOUS POSSIBILITY IN ITS *SUSPECT SCAN*.
TEK

SECURITY GUARD AT THE BANK ISN'T ALL HE SEEMS. CONVICTION FOR THEFT IN '79, SERVED TWO YEARS FOR FRAUD IN '82.
USED AN ASSUMED NAME AND FORGED REFERENCES TO GET THE JOB.

WHAT DO YOU THINK?
HMM. A SECURITY GUARD'S *UN*LIKELY TO HAVE ACCESS TO THE BANK'S *DATA CODES*.

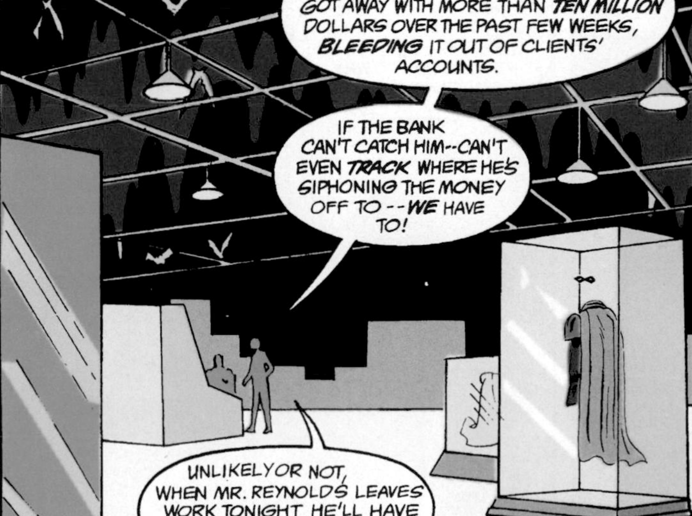
STILL, THIS COMPUTER FRAUDSTER'S GOT AWAY WITH MORE THAN *TEN MILLION* DOLLARS OVER THE PAST FEW WEEKS, *BLEEDING* IT OUT OF CLIENTS' ACCOUNTS.
IF THE BANK CAN'T CATCH HIM--CAN'T EVEN *TRACK* WHERE HE'S SIPHONING THE MONEY OFF TO --*WE* HAVE TO!
UNLIKELY OR NOT, WHEN MR. REYNOLDS LEAVES WORK TONIGHT HE'LL HAVE *THE BATMAN* ON HIS CASE!

IN THE NAME OF PAPA LEGBA--
IN THE NAME OF BARON SAMEDI--
GREAT BAKA, ACCEPT MY HUMBLE OFFERINGS.

FEED ON MY DEVOTION.
GROW STRONG ON MY PRAYERS.
DRAW POWER FROM MY GIFTS.

FEED THAT POWER BACK TO ME! GIVE ME STRENGTH TO CARRY OUT MY PART. LET ME GAIN FAVOR IN THE EYES OF MY DARK LORD OBEAH!

GREAT BAKA, GRANT ME--
PIERRE!

HOW MANY TIMES HAVE I TO TELL YOU, THIS IS NOT A TOY!
GIVE IT TO ME!

I'M SORRY, FATHER. I MEANT NO HARM.
I ONLY WONDERED... WHAT DO YOU KEEP IN THE CUPBOARD, THAT IT MUST STAY LOCKED? WHY CAN I NOT SEE...?

THAT IS MAN'S BUSINESS! WHEN YOU GROW UP, YOU WILL BE TOLD!
IT IS DANGEROUS--SO YOU NEVER GO NEAR IT! YOU HEAR? NEV--Ahuk!
AHUK!
HUKK! MY--AHUK!--MY MIXTURE! QUICKLY, BOY--AHUK!
HERE--
AHH, THAT'S BETTER...!
ASTHMA!
YOU KNOW YOU SHOULD NOT GET UPSET, FATHER. IT ALWAYS BRINGS ON AN ATTACK!
THEN YOU SHOULD NOT UPSET ME!
I MUST GO OUT NOW. EXPECT ME WHEN YOU SEE ME.

REMEMBER--YOU ARE A BOY. STAY AWAY FROM WHAT DOES NOT CONCERN YOU!

MAIL CALL, MASTER TIM!

IT WAS FORWARDED BY YOUR SCHOOL. NO DOUBT THEY THOUGHT ANYTHING URGENT MIGHT NOT WAIT TILL AFTER YOUR VACATION.
THANKS, ALFRED.
ANYTHING INTERESTING?
WE-ELL... AN INVITATION TO SCHOOL'S SUMMER BALL. MY LATEST BULLETIN FROM THE SHERLOCK HOLMES SOCIETY--
--AND A POSTCARD FROM MOM AND DAD!

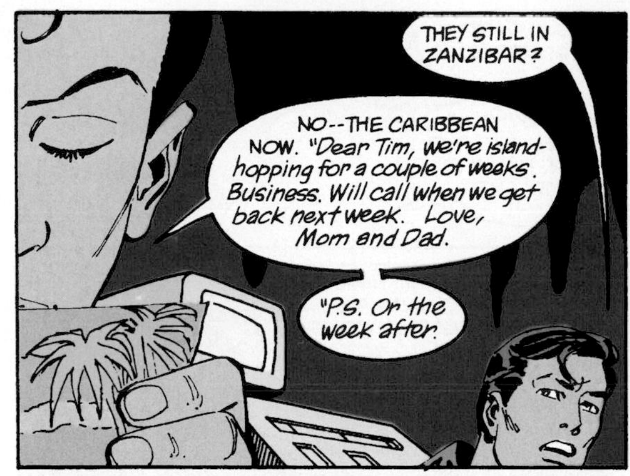

"--THEY CAN STAY AWAY FOR *MONTHS!*"
JEREMY, PLEASE INFORM *MRS. DRAKE* THAT IS *CAP HAITIEN*. ASK IF SHE'D LIKE TO TAKE A CLOSER LOOK.
CARIBHIRE T-R-1-1
YES, MR. DRAKE.

ER, MRS. DRAKE, YOUR HUSBAND SAYS--
I *HEARD*, JEREMY! TELL MR. DRAKE *NO*, I DO *NOT* WANT TO TAKE A CLOSER LOOK AT HAITI!

ALSO TELL HIM THAT IF HE'D BOTHERED TO READ THE FILE I PREPARED, HE'D KNOW THERE'S NO POINT.
THE EUPHORIA AT THE OVERTHROW OF THE DUVALIERS IS LONG GONE. THE MILITARY CLINGS TO POWER. THE PEOPLE LIVE IN FEAR AND POVERTY AND SUPERSTITION!
KINDLY INFORM MY WIFE IT IS PRECISELY BECAUSE OF THE INSTABILITY THAT HAITI NEEDS NEW ENTERPRISES!
AND TELL MY HUSBAND THAT VOODOO AND FREE MARKET CAPITALISM JUST DO NOT MIX!
AS I'VE SAID ALL ALONG, WE SHOULD SETTLE FOR JAMAICA!
TANGO-RED-11. COME IN, TANGO-RED-11.
THIS IS TANGO-RED. WHAT CAN I DO FOR YOU?
YOU CAN LAND YOUR AIRCRAFT BELOW. NOW.
WHAT? DON'T BE ABSURD! WHO IS THIS?
I AM THE OBEAH MAN.
I--I HAVE HEARD OF YOU. WH-WHAT DO YOU WANT WITH ME?
LAND YOUR PLANE, M. GOOSSENS.
YOU SEE, I KNOW YOUR NAME. I KNOW YOUR HOUSE.
I KNOW YOUR BARBER.
I KNOW THAT YOU BELIEVE!

I HAVE MADE A DOLL, M. GOOSSENS. IT IS YOU.
I AM GOING TO HURT THE DOLL, MONSIEUR. I AM GOING TO HURT YOU.
BADLY.
VERY, VERY BADLY.
YOUR EYES, MONSIEUR.
WHAT'S THAT, PILOT? IS SOMETHING WRONG?
N-NO! PLEASE--DON'T!
I...I'LL DO WHATEVER YOU WANT!
PILOT!
WHAT THE HELL ARE YOU DOING?
RRRRRRRRRRR

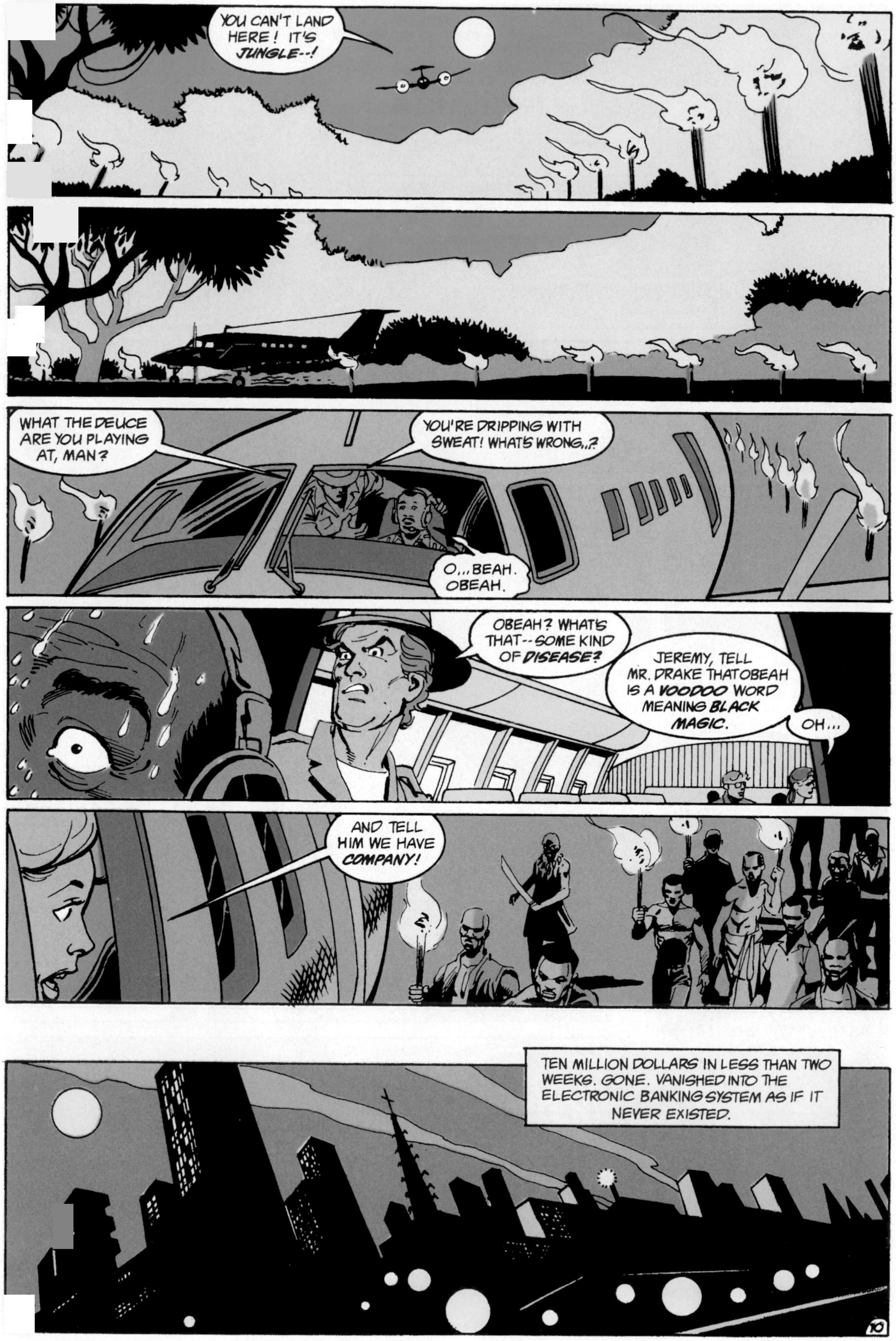

YOU CAN'T LAND HERE! IT'S *JUNGLE*--!

WHAT THE DEUCE ARE YOU PLAYING AT, MAN?

YOU'RE DRIPPING WITH SWEAT! WHAT'S WRONG..?

O... BEAH. OBEAH.

OBEAH? WHAT'S THAT--SOME KIND OF *DISEASE*?

JEREMY, TELL MR. DRAKE THAT OBEAH IS A *VOODOO* WORD MEANING *BLACK MAGIC*.

OH...

AND TELL HIM WE HAVE *COMPANY*!

REYNOLDS' PAST FORM DOESN'T INDICATE HE HAS THE KNOWLEDGE TO DO IT.
FIRST GOTHAM BANK
SEE YOU IN THE MORNING, DUNC!
SPSH
BUT MAYBE HE KNOWS A MAN WHO HAS!
ENDA TH' ROAD, DUNC.
WHAT THE HECK--?
YOU PICKED THE WRONG GUY TO STRONG-ARM, PUNKS! I'LL--
KRAK!
AAAAGH!
M--MY WRIST...! YOU... BROKE MY WRIST...!
WHY, SO I DID!
SADLY FOR YOU, IT MAY ONLY BE THE START.
RECOGNIZE THIS?
N-NO... I--

WILLY THE HAT AND HIS CREW. DRUG MERCHANTS. AND NONE TOO PLEASED WITH REYNOLD, IT SEEMS!
KRAK
LET ME REFRESH YOUR MEMORY, DUNC. IT'S SOLID GOLD. COST ME CLOSE ON A HUNDRED THOU.
SO VALUABLE I PUT IT IN FIRST GOTHAM'S SECURITY VAULT. AND GUESS WHAT, DUNC...?
LAST NIGHT PLASTIC SAM--YOU KNOW, THE FENCE?--TRIED TO SELL IT BACK TO ME!
OUFF!
SO REYNOLDS IS RAIDING FIRST'S VAULTS AND SELLING THE PROCEEDS. NOTHING TO DO WITH MY COMPUTER CASE.
CAN'T COMPLAIN, THOUGH--
NOVICK FIRE ESCAPE, INC
KLUNGGG
THERE'LL BE SIX FEWER CREEPS ON THE STREETS TOMORROW!
ZUNGG

AGH!
CHOK

SWIITT
CHAK

KEEP BACK, BATMAN! YOU HAVE NO QUARREL WITH ME!
CHAT
WRONG, WILLY--
SPTASH

I HAVE A QUARREL WITH EVERY PIECE OF STREET-SLIME WHO PEDDLES DEATH TO BUY GOLD! TELL THAT TO YOUR JEWELER--
--WHEN YOU GET OUT OF JAIL!
SWAK

YOU CHOSE THE WRONG STRONGBOX, REYNOLDS TOUGH LUCK.
NOW-- IF YOU'LL TELL ME WHERE I CAN FIND THIS PLASTIC SAM...

CARIBHIRE T-R-1-1

YOU CAN'T DO THAT! THAT'S A MILLION-DOLLAR AIRPLANE!
WE DO WHAT WE WANT.

NOW BE SILENT!
WAK!

FRUMPH
KRONCH
FRATCH
KRAKK!
SPSH

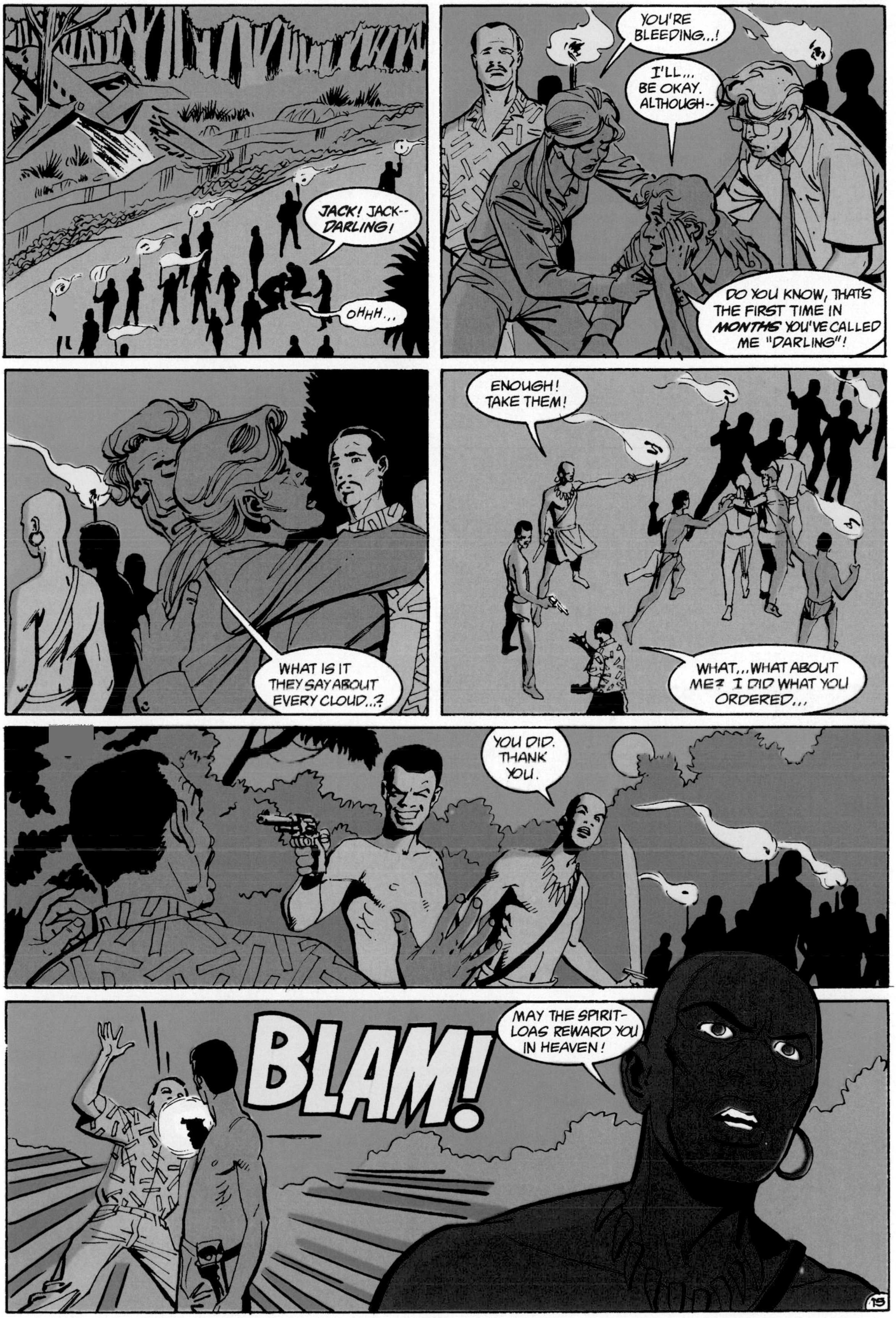

YOU DID. THANK YOU.

BLAM!

MAY THE SPIRIT-LOAS REWARD YOU IN HEAVEN!

THEY... THEY'VE SHOT THE PILOT!
MR. DRAKE--YOU HAVE TO DO SOMETHING! THEY'LL KILL US ALL!

I DON'T WANT TO DIE! I DON'T WANT TO!
STAY CALM, MAN!
OBVIOUSLY THEY WANT US ALIVE. THE PILOT WAS... SUPERFLUOUS TO THEIR REQUIREMENTS.

JUST KEEP YOUR HEAD. DON'T PANIC. WE'LL PULL THR--
MOVE!

BUT THIS IS CRAZY! YOU AND MRS. DRAKE ARE HEADS OF A MULTI-MILLION DOLLAR COMPANY! I'M YOUR PERSONAL SECRETARY, FOR GOODNESS' SAKE!
THEY CAN'T JUST... KIDNAP US LIKE THIS!

THEY HAVE.
WE'RE IN THEIR JUNGLE NOW, JEREMY. WE PLAY BY THEIR RULES!

WHEREVER WE'RE GOING, I THINK WE'VE ARRIVED!

WELCOME TO HAITI, MR. AND MRS. DRAKE. I AM YOUR HOST.

I AM THE OBEAH MAN.

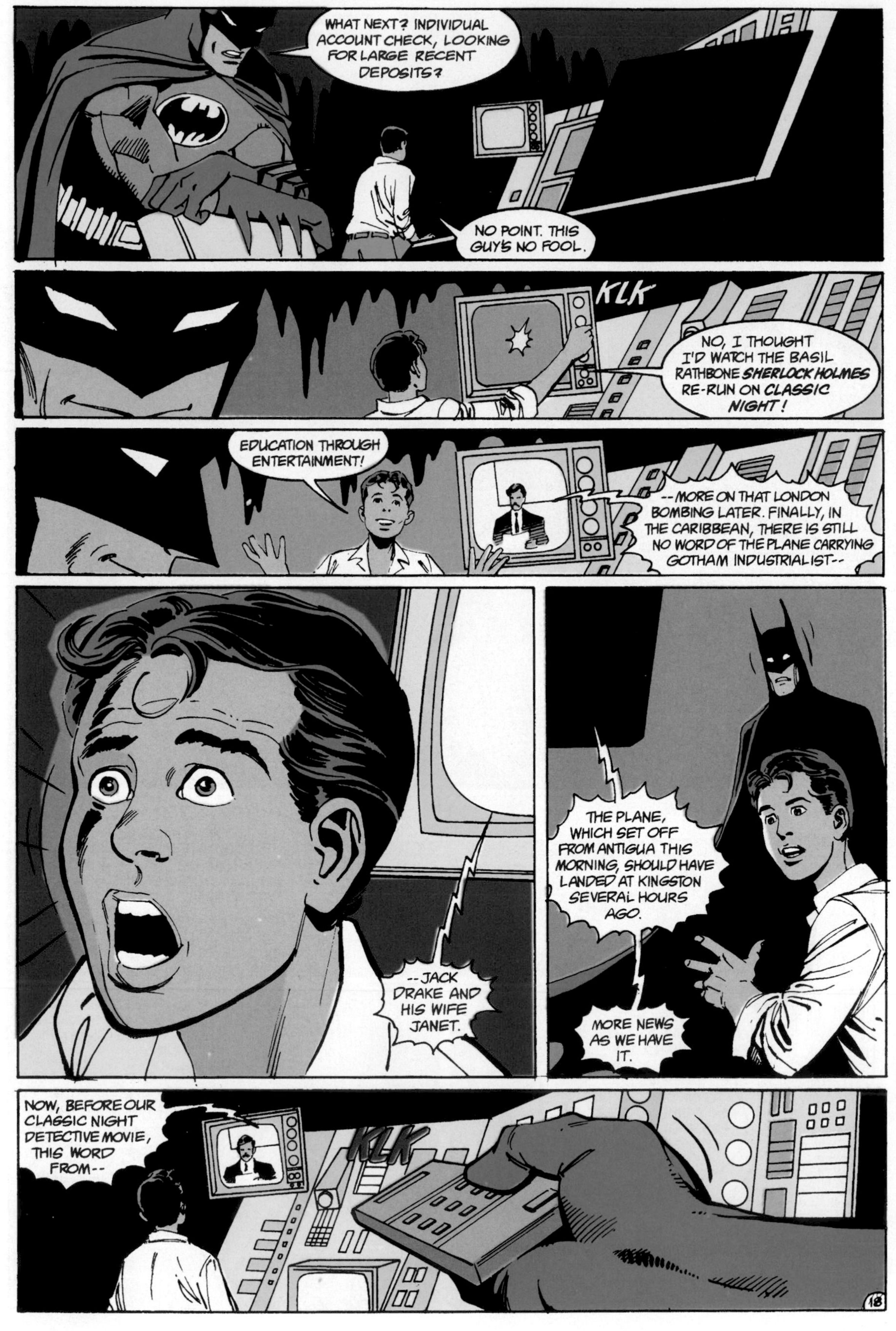
WHAT NEXT? INDIVIDUAL ACCOUNT CHECK, LOOKING FOR LARGE RECENT DEPOSITS?
NO POINT. THIS GUY'S NO FOOL.
KLK
NO, I THOUGHT I'D WATCH THE BASIL RATHBONE SHERLOCK HOLMES RE-RUN ON CLASSIC NIGHT!
EDUCATION THROUGH ENTERTAINMENT!
--MORE ON THAT LONDON BOMBING LATER. FINALLY, IN THE CARIBBEAN, THERE IS STILL NO WORD OF THE PLANE CARRYING GOTHAM INDUSTRIALIST--
--JACK DRAKE AND HIS WIFE JANET.
THE PLANE, WHICH SET OFF FROM ANTIGUA THIS MORNING, SHOULD HAVE LANDED AT KINGSTON SEVERAL HOURS AGO.
MORE NEWS AS WE HAVE IT.
NOW, BEFORE OUR CLASSIC NIGHT DETECTIVE MOVIE, THIS WORD FROM--
KLK

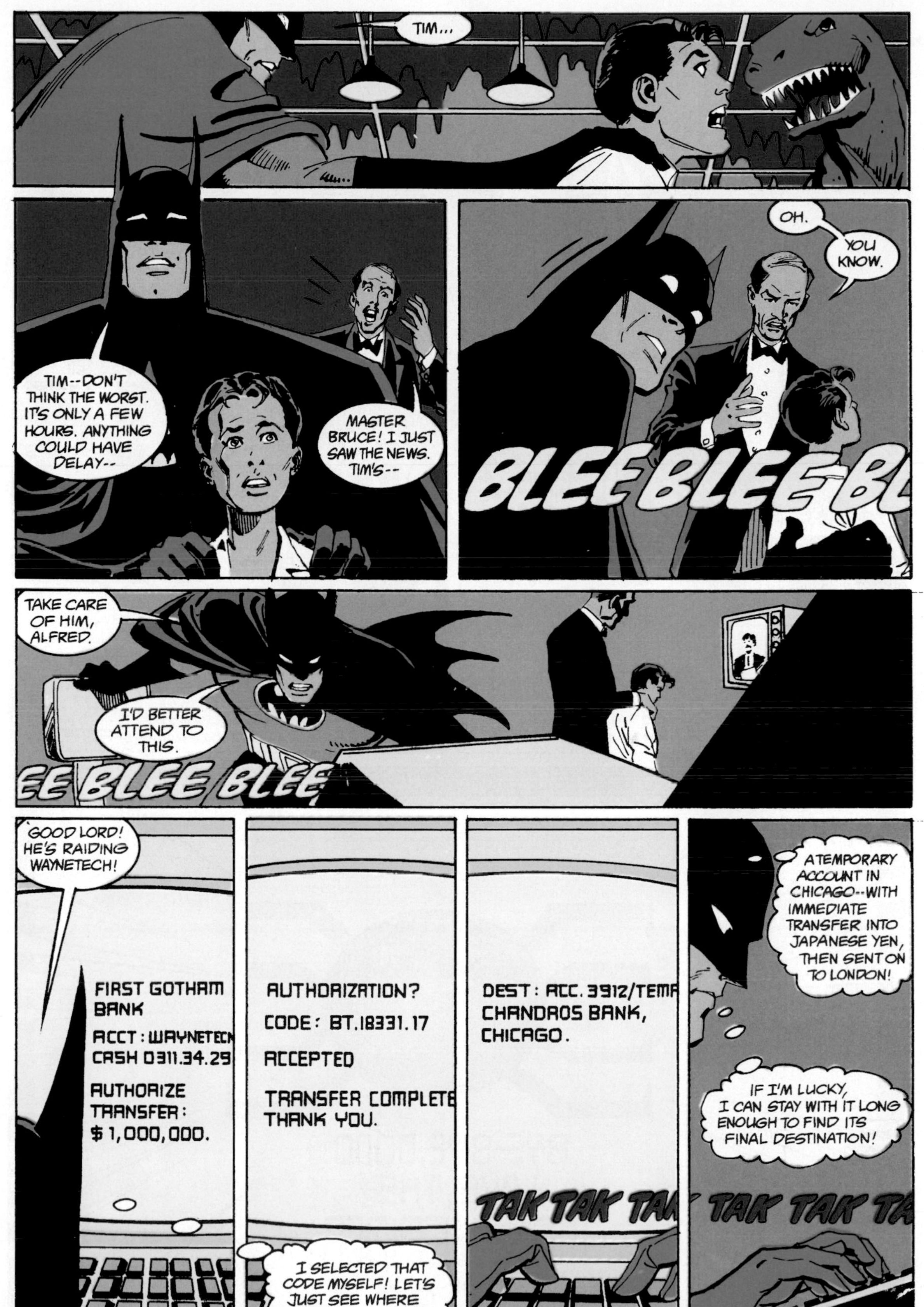
TIM...
TIM--DON'T THINK THE WORST. IT'S ONLY A FEW HOURS. ANYTHING COULD HAVE DELAY--
MASTER BRUCE! I JUST SAW THE NEWS. TIM'S--
OH.
YOU KNOW.
BLEE BLEE
TAKE CARE OF HIM, ALFRED.
I'D BETTER ATTEND TO THIS.
EE BLEE BLEE
GOOD LORD! HE'S RAIDING WAYNETECH!
FIRST GOTHAM BANK
ACCT : WAYNETECH
CASH 0311.34.29
AUTHORIZE TRANSFER :
$ 1,000,000.
AUTHORIZATION?
CODE : BT.18331.17
ACCEPTED
TRANSFER COMPLETE
THANK YOU.
I SELECTED THAT CODE MYSELF! LET'S JUST SEE WHERE THE MONEY'S GOING...
DEST : ACC. 3912/TEMP
CHANDROS BANK,
CHICAGO.
TAK TAK TAK TAK TAK
A TEMPORARY ACCOUNT IN CHICAGO--WITH IMMEDIATE TRANSFER INTO JAPANESE YEN, THEN SENT ON TO LONDON!
IF I'M LUCKY, I CAN STAY WITH IT LONG ENOUGH TO FIND ITS FINAL DESTINATION!

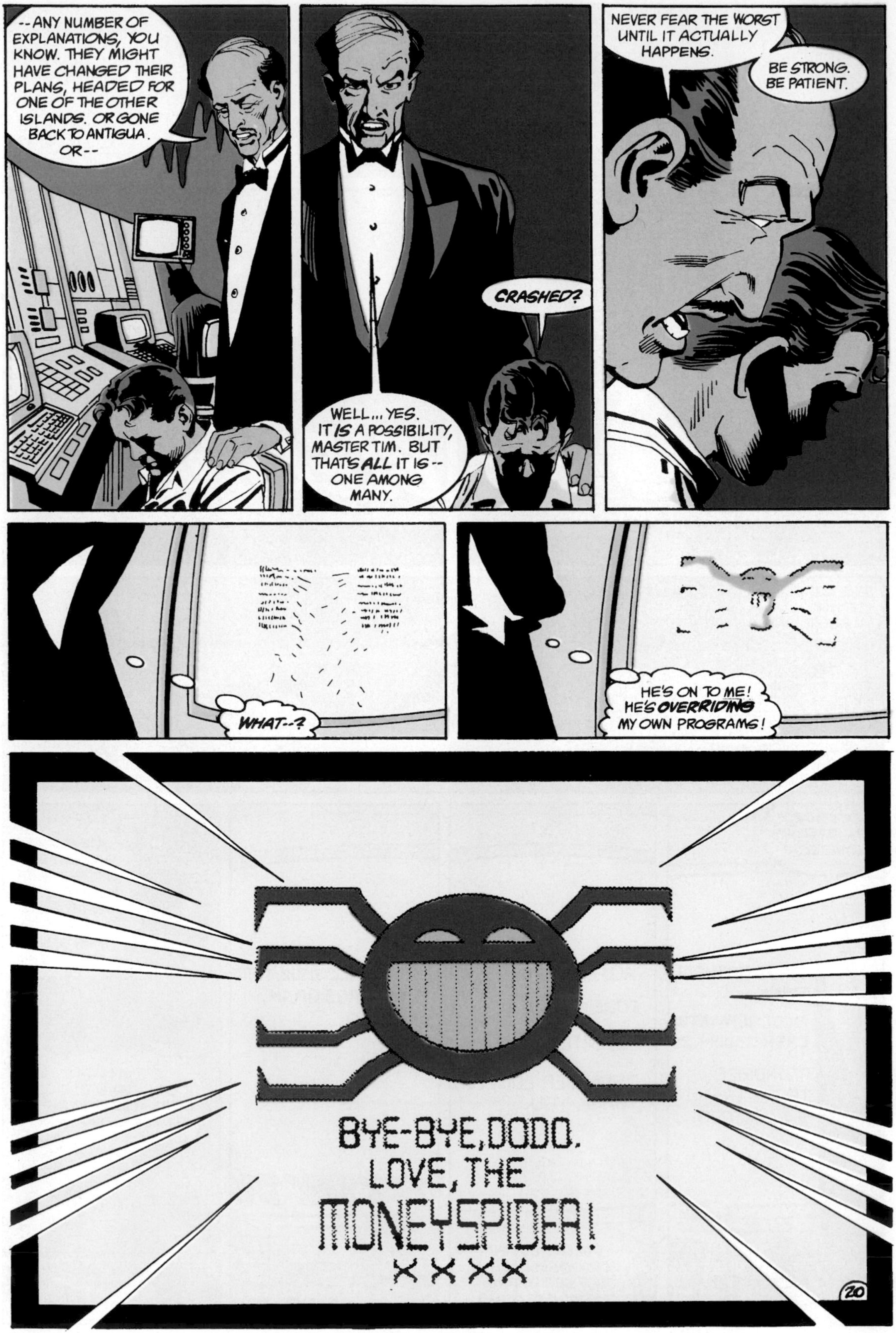

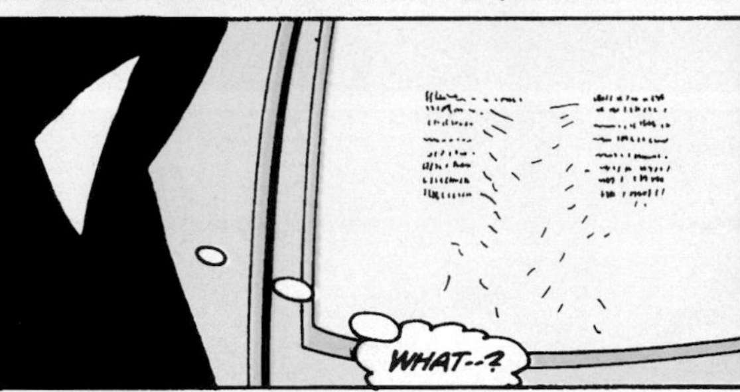

BYE-BYE, DODO.
LOVE, THE
MONEYSPIDER!
XXXX

SORRY ABOUT THAT, TIM. I HAD TO--
THAT'S ALL RIGHT.

IF YOU WANT ME, I'LL BE IN MY ROOM.
TIM--!
SIR! IF I MAY BE SO BOLD...!

IT MAY BE WISER TO LEAVE HIM FOR A WHILE. HE NEEDS TO BE ABLE TO...ADJUST.
AND IF THE WORST DOES COME TO THE WORST...

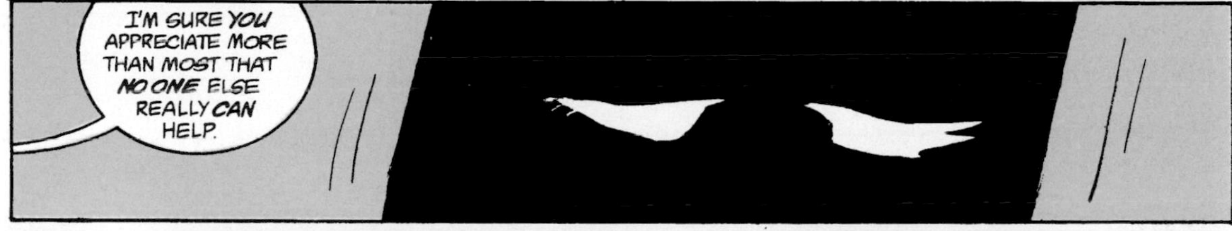
I'M SURE YOU APPRECIATE MORE THAN MOST THAT NO ONE ELSE REALLY CAN HELP.

I HAVE TO BE STRONG. I HAVE TO BE PATIENT.

I HAVE TO BE THERE WHEN HE NEEDS ME.
HE FORGOT TO TELL ME--
--DO HEROES CRY?
NEXT ISSUE: BEYOND BELIEF!

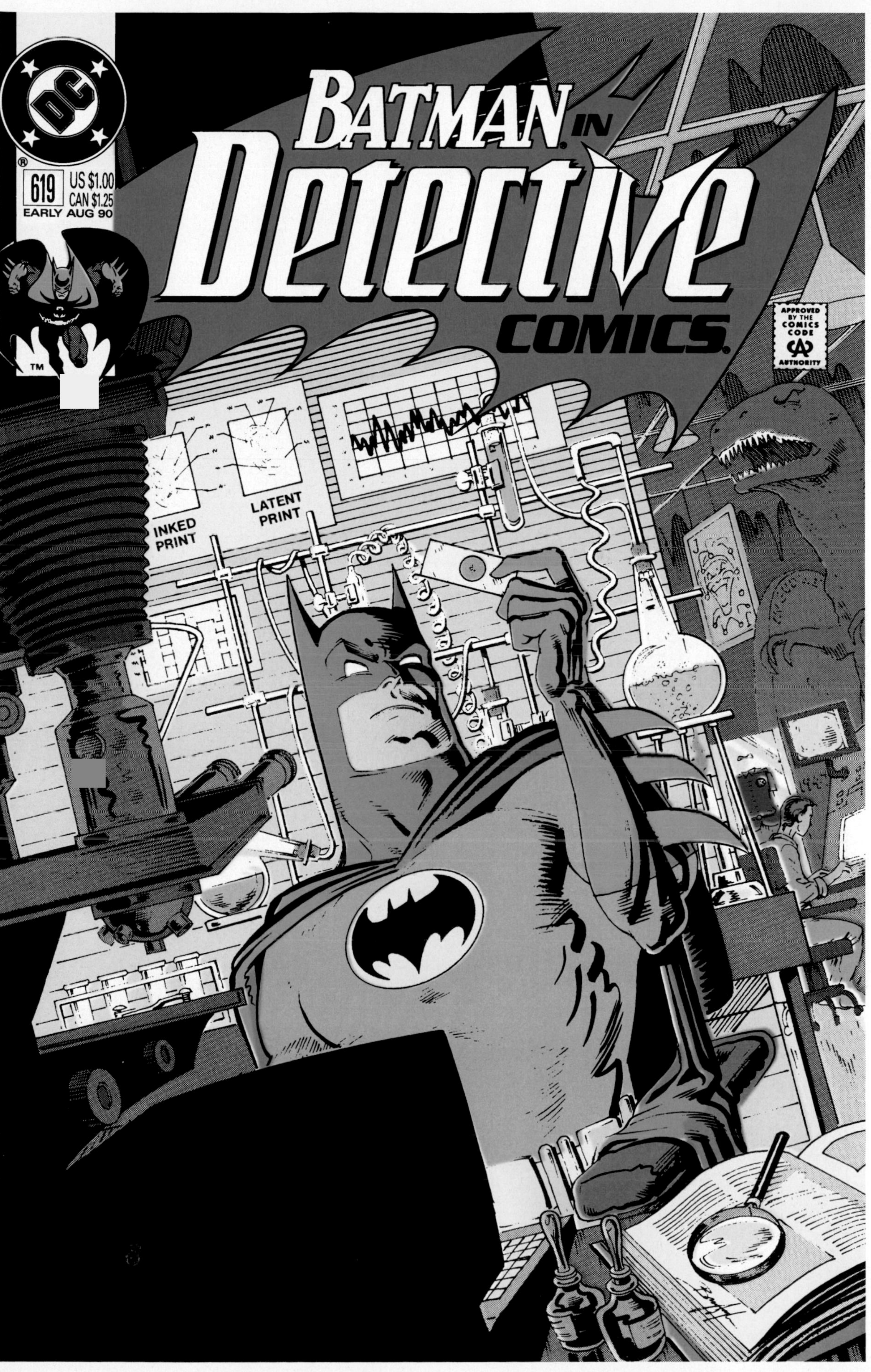
DC
619
US $1.00
CAN $1.25
EARLY AUG 90
BATMAN IN
Detective
COMICS
APPROVED BY THE COMICS CODE AUTHORITY
INKED PRINT
LATENT PRINT

Cover art by Norm Breyfogle

RITE of PASSAGE
PART TWO: BEYOND BELIEF!
YOU--YOU INHUMAN BRUTE! THAT WAS MURDER-- COLD-BLOODED, VICIOUS MURDER!
ALAN GRANT SCRIPT
NORM BREYFOGLE PENCILLER
STEVE MITCHELL INKER
ADRIENNE ROY COLORIST
TODD KLEIN LETTERER
DAN RASPLER ASSOC. EDITOR
DENNIS O'NEIL EDITOR
BATMAN CREATED BY BOB KANE

I'LL SEE YOU PAY! DAMN YOU--IF IT TAKES EVERY CENT I OWN AND THE REST OF MY LIFE TO DO IT, I'LL SEE YOU PAY!
MR. DRAKE, EVERY CENT YOU OWN WILL SOON BE MINE.

AND AS FOR YOUR LIFESPAN--DO NOT COUNT ON IT BEING A LONG ONE IF YOUR COMPANY FAILS TO PAY YOUR RANSOM!

BUT DO NOT WORRY. I AM SURE THAT, ONCE THEY SEE THIS FILM, THEY, TOO, WILL REALIZE-- THE OBEAH MAN MAKES NO IDLE THREATS!

YOU THINK THIS WILL WORK, LOUIS DANGE? WILL WE BE RICH--OR MERELY THE NEXT SET OF BODIES FOUND BURNING AT THE SIDE OF THE ROAD?
HOW CAN YOU DOUBT?

YOU KNOW THE POWER OF THE OBEAH MAN AS WELL AS I. HE COMMANDS POWERFUL SPIRITS.
IF WE BELIEVE IN HIM, HE CANNOT FAIL!

YOU SPEAK TRUE, LOUIS DANGE. IN MATTERS OF THE SPIRIT, BELIEF IS ALWAYS THE KEY!
MARK IT WELL, ALL OF YOU, FOR ONE DAY BELIEF--OR ITS LACK--WILL MEAN YOUR LIFE ...OR YOUR DEATH!

HERE--TAKE THIS TO MALICIEN AT THE AIRPORT. TELL HIM TO PROCEED AS PLANNED.
AT ONCE, MY LORD!

HENRI--MARSAL--INSIDE!
THERE IS A... MESS REQUIRES CLEANING.

OH, JACK...! IT--IT'S HORRIBLE! POOR JEREMY! I--I JUST CAN'T BELIEVE THEY WOULD...
THERE, DARLING! PLEASE--I KNOW IT'S HARD, BUT TRY TO STAY IN CONTROL!

WE'VE NO OPTION BUT TO SEE THIS THROUGH--TAKE IT ONE STEP AT A TIME!

"EVERYTHING'S DOWN TO WHAT HAPPENS IN GOTHAM!"
--SORRY, MR. WAYNE. THE SEARCH WAS CALLED OFF FOR THE NIGHT.

THERE ARE TWO CHOPPERS HEADING OUT RIGHT NOW, AND ALL SHIPPING HAS BEEN ASKED TO KEEP A LOOKOUT. OUR HOPES ARE HIGH!
THANK YOU. PLEASE KEEP ME INFORMED OF ANY DEVELOPMENTS.

ALFRED--!

I'LL TAKE IT TO HIM.
VERY GOOD, SIR. I THINK HE'LL APPRECIATE THAT.

TIM!

I'M AFRAID NOT. BUT THEY'VE RESUMED THE SEARCH. THEY'LL FIND THEM.

WILL THEY?

WE CAN ONLY HOPE.

DON'T BROOD TOO MUCH, SON. FOR YOUR PARENTS' *SAKE*, BE STRONG. ALWAYS REMEMBER-- LIFE HAS TO GO ON.

DO YOU WANT ME TO TAKE THE DAY OFF TO BE WITH YOU?

NO. IT'S OKAY. DEEP DOWN I KNOW YOU'RE RIGHT. ALL I CAN DO IS ***WAIT***.

Sometimes in the night I hear the shriek of splintering wood.

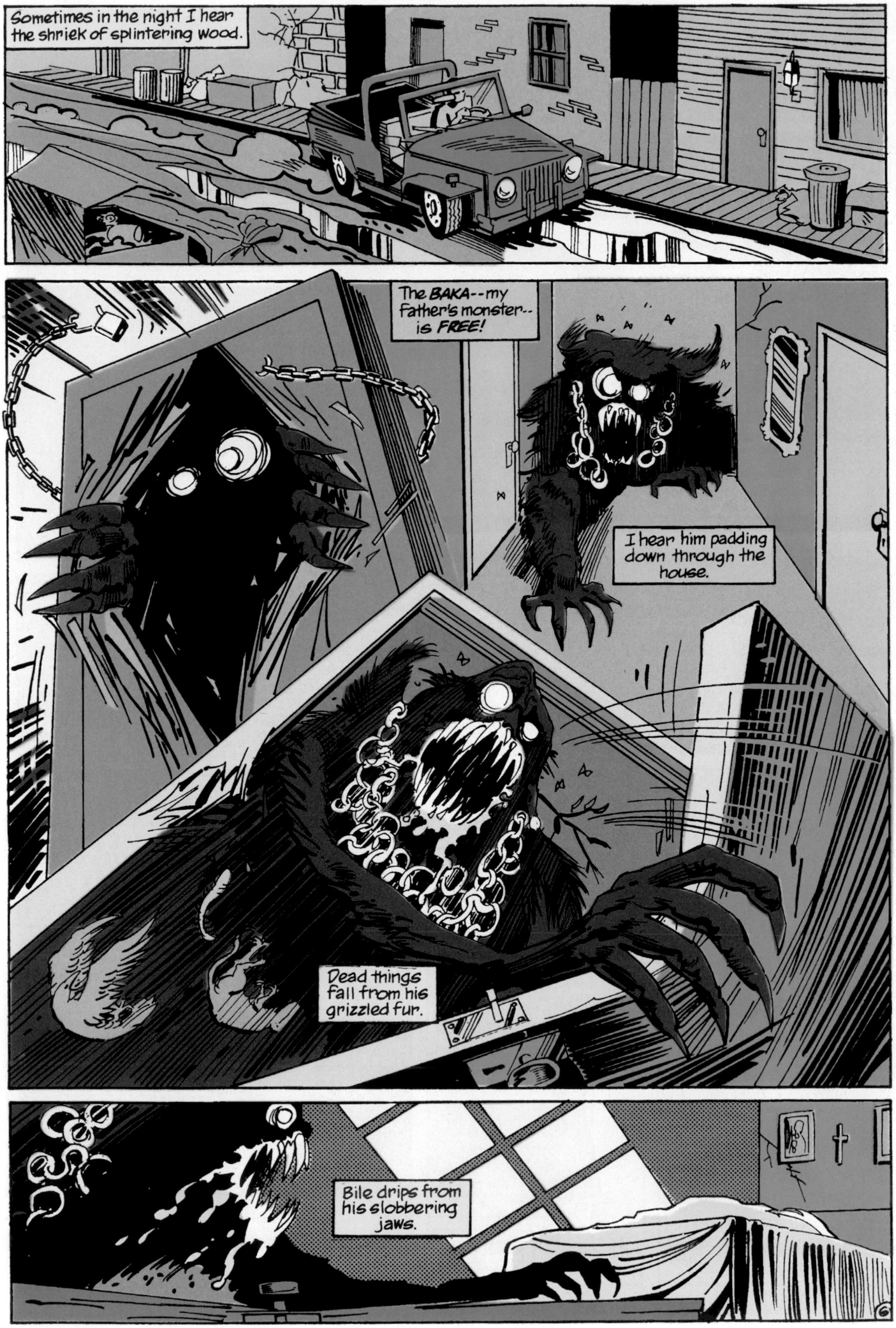

The BAKA--my father's monster-- is FREE!
I hear him padding down through the house.
Dead things fall from his grizzled fur.

Bile drips from his slobbering jaws.

He thinks I don't believe in him! He's coming for me! He's coming--
N-NO! NO--!
NO! DON'T HURT ME! DON'T HURT ME!

PIERRE! PIERRE!
FA-FATHER...?

I... HAD A NIGHTMARE. THERE WAS A MONSTER--THE BAKA! IT WANTED TO KILL ME...!
I TOLD YOU, BOY-- BAKA IS NONE OF YOUR BUSINESS!

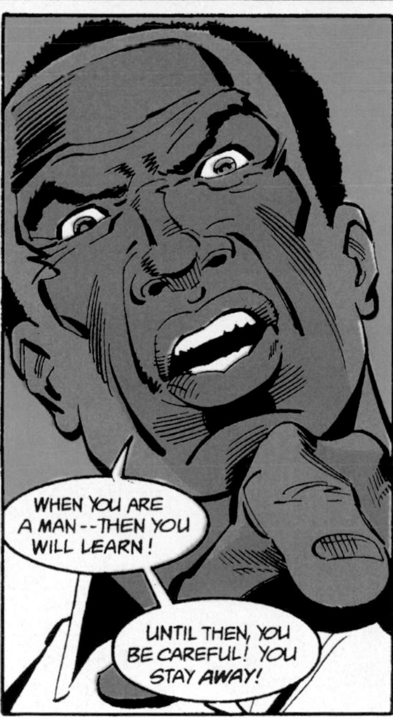
WHEN YOU ARE A MAN--THEN YOU WILL LEARN!
UNTIL THEN, YOU BE CAREFUL! YOU STAY AWAY!

I HAVE HAD A LONG NIGHT. I NEED REST.
GO AND VISIT YOUR FRIENDS OR SOMETHING!

SUNSET. NO WORD FROM THE CARIBBEAN.
I KNOW EXACTLY HOW THE BOY FEELS. ALL THOSE YEARS AGO, AND STILL THE PAIN SMOLDERS.

ARCADE
YET, I FIND IT HARD TO BE NATURAL WITH HIM. ALMOST AS IF... I'M AFRAID.
THIEVES! COME BACK!

HELP! POLICE-- AAAAH!
AH, SHUDDIT, LOUDMOUTH!
BAM!
THE LIVES OF TOO MANY CLOSE TO ME HAVE BEEN BLIGHTED BY TRAGEDY.
UP THERE--!

BLAM
BLAM
BLAM
MAKES ME WONDER SOMETIMES IF I'M JINXED

WHERE'D HE--?
ENOUGH!

THE COWL AND THE CAPE SAY I DON'T THINK LIKE THAT. I CAN'T AFFORD TO.
OOF!

IN THE NIGHT I WALK THE FINE LINE--
SPEEOW
SPANG
THT
BLAM
BLAM
CHK
SKT
STAY STILL--!

PTANNG
SHAK
SPTAK
THE EDGE--
ANNGHH!
AAAH!
BLAM
SLAM

AND TRAGEDY'S FOR OTHER MEN!
--WAS HANDED IN TO DRAKE INDUSTRIES THIS AFTERNOON.
GOTHAM POLICE
BE WARNED-- IT'S NOT PRETTY.
MY FRIENDS--JACK AND JANET DRAKE HAVE BEEN TAKEN CAPTIVE BY THE CARIBBEAN ECONOMIC FRONT.

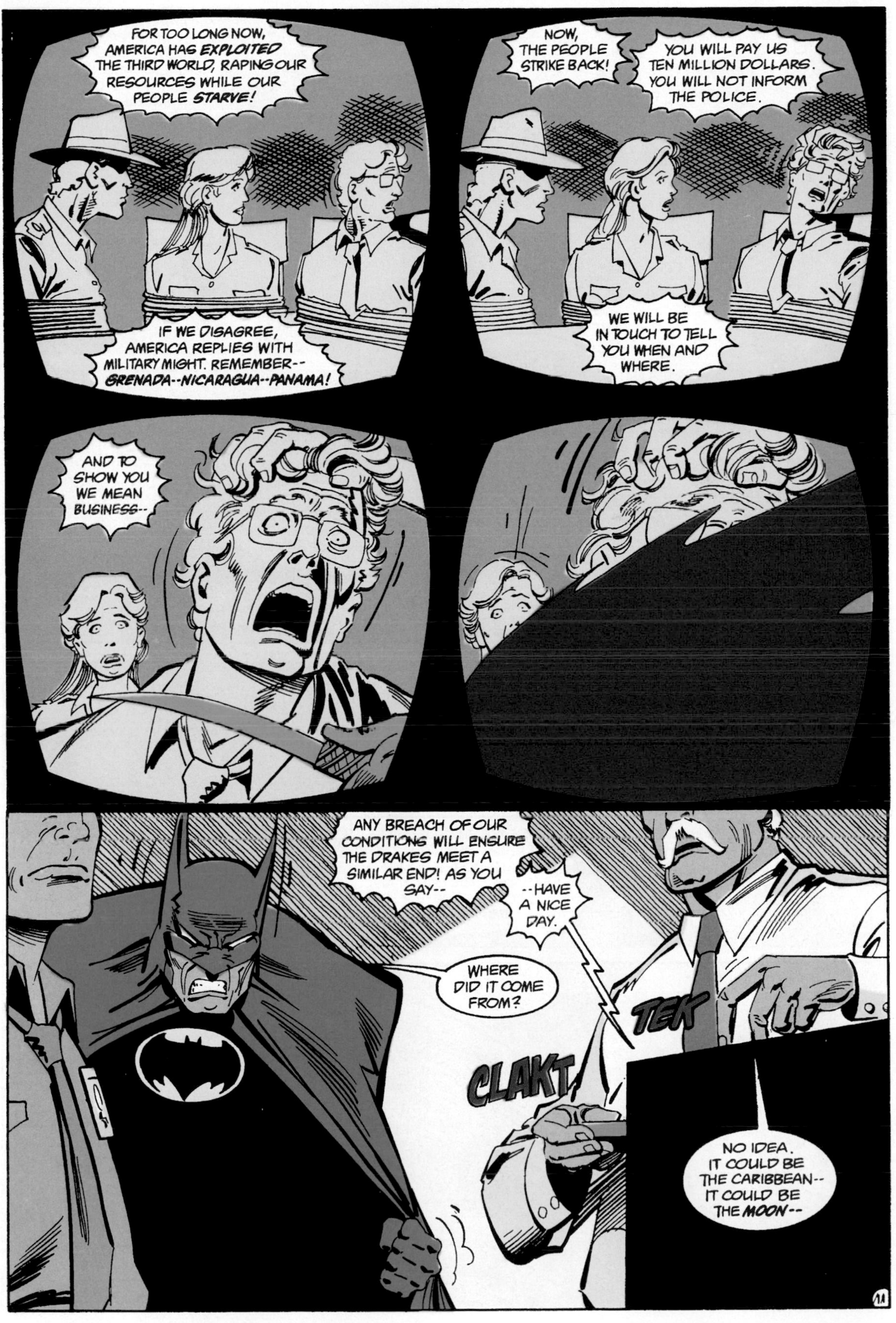

FOR TOO LONG NOW, AMERICA HAS EXPLOITED THE THIRD WORLD, RAPING OUR RESOURCES WHILE OUR PEOPLE STARVE!
IF WE DISAGREE, AMERICA REPLIES WITH MILITARY MIGHT. REMEMBER-- GRENADA--NICARAGUA--PANAMA!
NOW, THE PEOPLE STRIKE BACK!
YOU WILL PAY US TEN MILLION DOLLARS. YOU WILL NOT INFORM THE POLICE.
WE WILL BE IN TOUCH TO TELL YOU WHEN AND WHERE.
AND TO SHOW YOU WE MEAN BUSINESS--
ANY BREACH OF OUR CONDITIONS WILL ENSURE THE DRAKES MEET A SIMILAR END! AS YOU SAY--
--HAVE A NICE DAY.
WHERE DID IT COME FROM?
TEK
CLAKT
NO IDEA. IT COULD BE THE CARIBBEAN-- IT COULD BE THE MOON--

THEY COULD BE HOLDING HIM IN--
PUFF PUFF
--GOTHAM, FOR ALL WE KNOW!
IT ARRIVED IN A PLAIN WRAPPER. STANDARD DOMESTIC VIDEO TAPE. FORENSIC SAYS IT'S BEEN WIPED OF PRINTS.
HMM. A FAINT ODOR...?
SO FORENSIC SAID. THEY DON'T KNOW WHAT, THOUGH. CAN'T SAY I NOTICED IT MYSELF.
YOU MIGHT, IF SMOKING HADN'T DESTROYED YOUR SENSE OF SMELL!
ALL RIGHT IF I...?
BE MY GUEST. I'VE HAD COPIES MADE.
HAVE THEY HEARD AGAIN AT DRAKE--ABOUT THE RANSOM?
NO. SAY THEY DON'T KNOW IF THEY'RE GOING TO PAY UP, EITHER.
DRAKE HIMSELF MADE THE RULE--ANY KIDNAP TO BE REPORTED TO THE POLICE, NO RANSOM TO BE PAID IN ANY CIRCUMSTANCE FOR ANY EMPLOYEE!
I SEE HIS POINT. PAY UP ONCE AND YOU OPEN THE WAY TO A FLOOD OF EXECUTIVE KIDNAPPINGS.
YET IF THEY DON'T--WELL, THESE PEOPLE AREN'T JOKING!
12

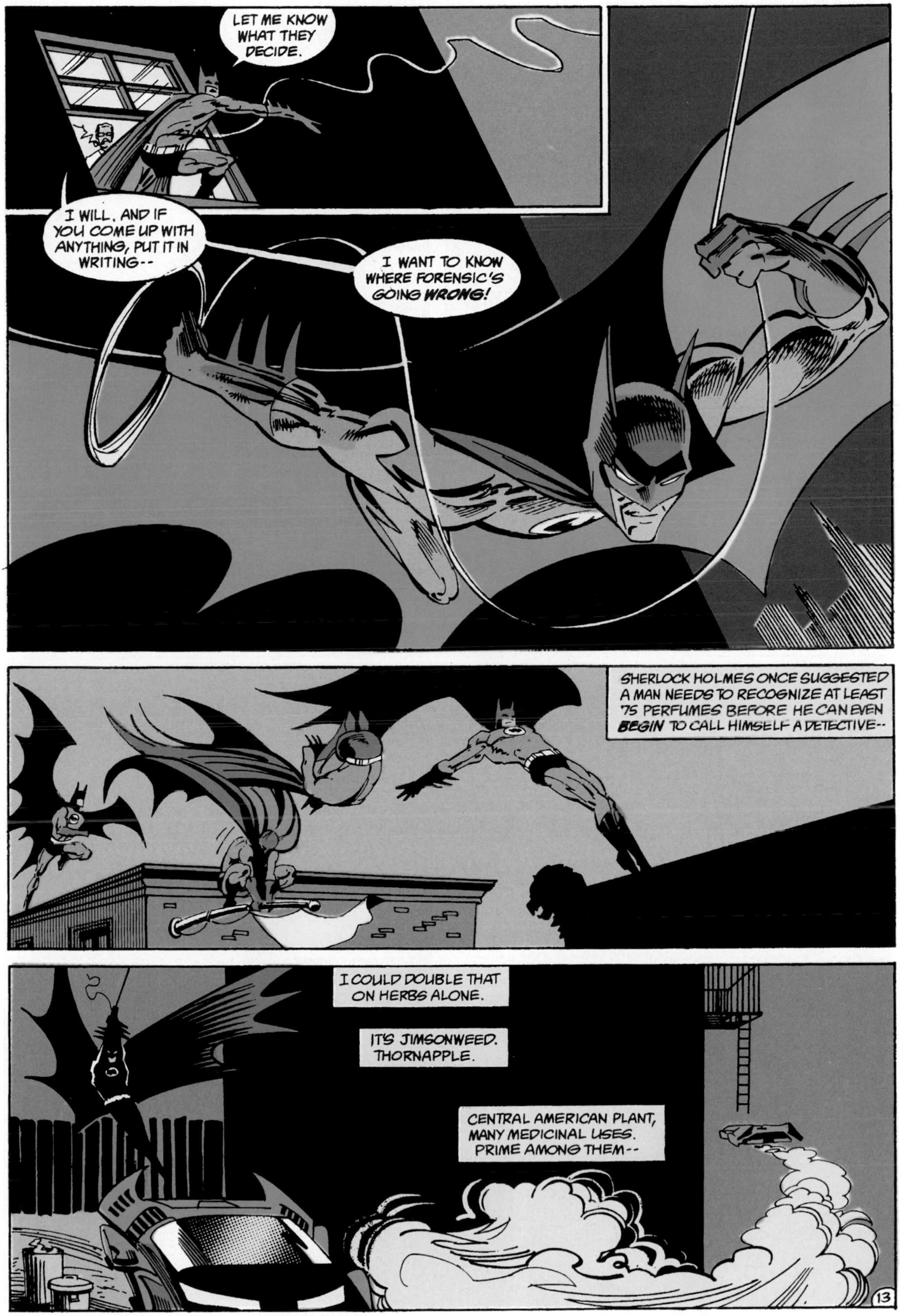

LET ME KNOW WHAT THEY DECIDE.

I WILL. AND IF YOU COME UP WITH ANYTHING, PUT IT IN WRITING--

I WANT TO KNOW WHERE FORENSIC'S GOING **WRONG**!

"AROMATIC SMOKING MIXTURE FOR ASTHMA RELIEF."
AHUK! AHUK!

--DO YOU THINK, RAYMOND? IS IT IN THERE?
I CAN'T HEAR ANYTHING...

MAYBE IF I KNOCK--
BOY! DON'T YOU DARE!

THIS IS YOUR LAST WARNING! KEEP AWAY FROM THAT CUPBOARD! IF I CATCH YOU HERE AGAIN, I WILL FORGET YOU ARE ONLY CHILDREN!
GO ON! CLEAR OFF!

DO YOU **REALLY** BELIEVE IN THE BAKA, PIERRE?
I... DON'T KNOW.

I USED TO BELIEVE THAT IF MY **HAIR** GOT WET WITH **DEW**, MY SPIRIT WOULD DISSOLVE. MY FATHER STILL DOES.
MINE'S JUST THE SAME. HE USED TO SAY THE **LOUPS-GAROUS** CAME OUT AT NIGHT, HUNTING--
--CHILDREN.
ULP!

WHERE IS HE, ALFRED?
IN THE CITY, SIR. HE HAS--
A JOB TO DO. YES, I KNOW.
MISSING PARENTS DON'T COME INTO IT, EH?

BE FAIR, SIR! MASTER BRUCE--
I'M SORRY. I'M JUST TIRED, I GUESS.
AND WORRIED AND FRUSTRATED AND FRAGILE!
GO ON-- YOU GET OFF TO BED. I'LL BRING YOU UP SOME COCOA.
THANKS, ALFRED.
EVEN IF I DON'T SEEM TO, I REALLY DO APPRECIATE YOU!
HE'S GONE. YOU CAN COME OUT NOW.
I THOUGHT YOU SAW ME COMING IN. FORTUNATELY, TIM DIDN'T.
BAD NEWS?
ABOUT AS BAD AS IT CAN BE. THEY'VE BEEN KIDNAPPED!
16

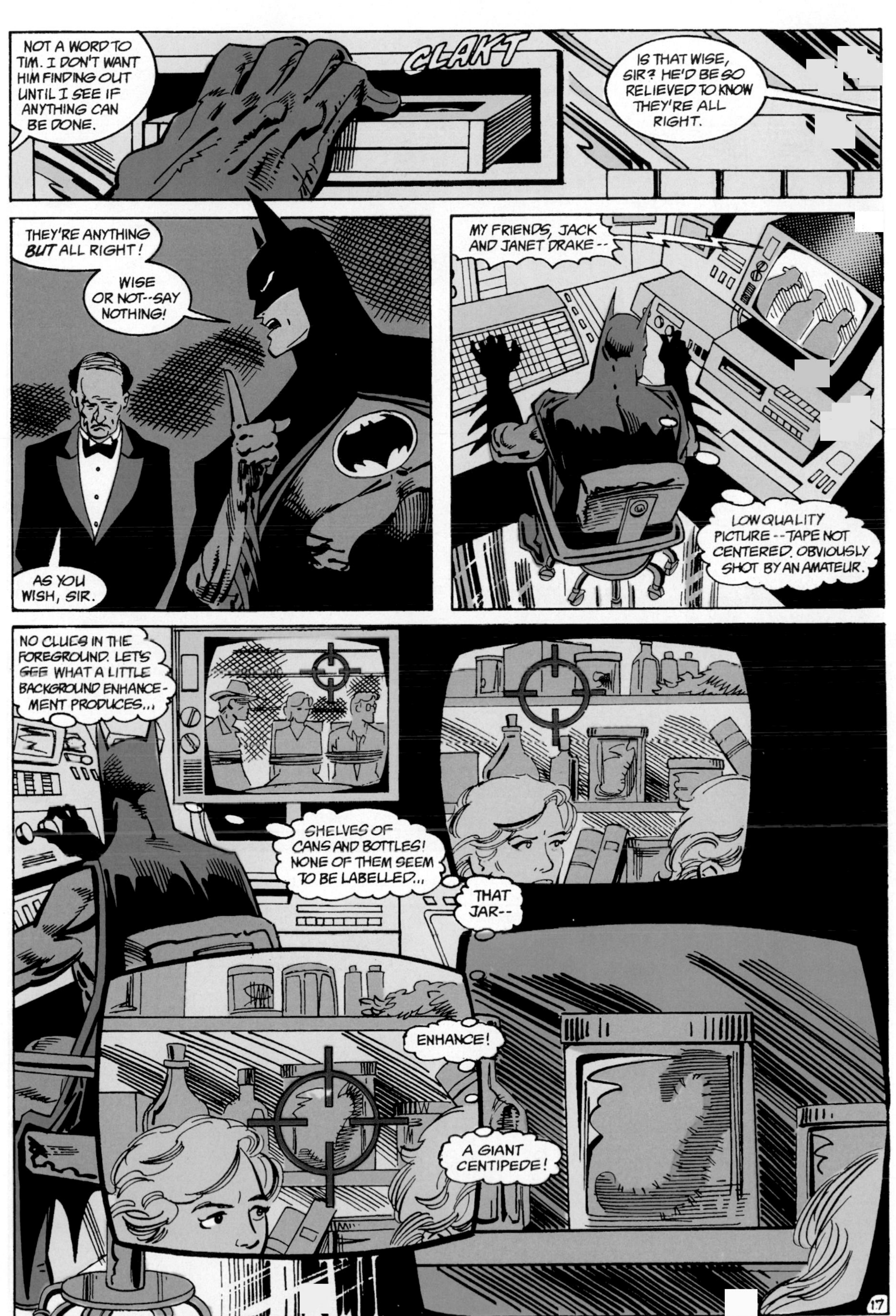
NOT A WORD TO TIM. I DON'T WANT HIM FINDING OUT UNTIL I SEE IF ANYTHING CAN BE DONE.
CLAKT
IS THAT WISE, SIR? HE'D BE SO RELIEVED TO KNOW THEY'RE ALL RIGHT.
THEY'RE ANYTHING BUT ALL RIGHT!
WISE OR NOT--SAY NOTHING!
AS YOU WISH, SIR.
MY FRIENDS, JACK AND JANET DRAKE--
LOW QUALITY PICTURE--TAPE NOT CENTERED. OBVIOUSLY SHOT BY AN AMATEUR.
NO CLUES IN THE FOREGROUND. LET'S SEE WHAT A LITTLE BACKGROUND ENHANCE-MENT PRODUCES...
SHELVES OF CANS AND BOTTLES! NONE OF THEM SEEM TO BE LABELLED...
THAT JAR--
ENHANCE!
A GIANT CENTIPEDE!

THAT'S A NEW ONE ON ME...

MYRIOPODA OF THE WORLD

HERE WE ARE... GIANT CARNIVOROUS CENTIPEDE. NATURAL HABITAT--

MYRIOPODA OF THE WORLD

BUT, LORD, WHAT IF THE AMERICANS DISOBEY? WHAT IF THEIR POLICE FIND OUT--?
EVEN IF THEY DO, THEY WILL BE LIKE MONKEYS CHASING THEIR OWN TAILS...

RUNNING FROM ISLAND TO ISLAND, COMBING THE CARIBBEAN FOR A GUERRILLA GROUP THAT DOES NOT EVEN EXIST.

--OF COURSE, IT WAS OUR DECISION TO GO WITH A NO-DEAL KIDNAP POLICY! BUT NOW THAT IT'S ACTUALLY HAPPENED--I WISH TO HELL WE HADN'T!

WHAT... WHAT DO YOU THINK? WILL THE BOARD AGREE TO PAY...?
RULES OR NOT, THEY'D BETTER.

I'LL FIRE THEM IF THEY DON'T!

SWAT
VOODOO
NOOOOO!
TIM...
THEY'RE STILL ALIVE! WHY DIDN'T YOU TELL ME? THEY'RE MY PARENTS! I'VE A RIGHT TO KNOW!
I DIDN'T WANT TO WORRY YOU NEEDLESSLY. THERE WAS NO POINT BUILDING UP YOUR HOPES IF... IF THERE'S NOTHING I CAN DO.
WORRY NEEDLESSLY? THEY'RE MY PARENTS. I THOUGHT THEY WERE DEAD!
GO AHEAD, GET IT OUT OF YOUR SYSTEM.
BAMP!

NO. I'M ALL RIGHT.
TELL ME WHAT YOU KNOW.

IN GOD WE
THE KIDNAPPERS CLAIM TO BE SOME NEW GUERRILLA OUTFIT-- BUT I THINK THAT'S ONLY A SMOKESCREEN.
UNLESS I READ IT WRONG, THEY'RE BEING HELD ON HAITI BY A VOODOO CULT!
VOODOO?
GIANT CENTIPEDE ON THE FILM. VOODOO SORCERERS --OR OBEAH MEN -- KEEP THEM AS A SYMBOL OF THEIR POWER.

SO... WE GO TO HAITI.
NO. IT'D BE LIKE SEARCHING FOR A NEEDLE IN A HAYSTACK. AND APART FROM ANYTHING ELSE, THE ISLAND'S MORE OR LESS UNDER MARTIAL LAW.

BRIIINGG
WE PLAY IT SLOW AND PATIENT. WE WAIT FOR THEIR RANSOM DEMAND, THEN PERHAPS--

BZZ
NEWS?
AFRAID NOT.
I HAVE TO GO OUT.

CLAK
CAN'T I SEE--?
NO. AND DON'T ASK WHY. JUST TRUST ME.

YOU RANG, SIR?
LOOK AFTER TIM. I'LL BE BACK AS SOON AS I CAN.

HE'S HANDLING IT WELL. BETTER THAN I EXPECTED. BUT HE'S HAD ENOUGH FOR ONE DAY. I COULDN'T TELL HIM THAT WAS GORDON--

DRAKE'S HAD THE *RANSOM CALL!*

STRANGE...
DICK GRAYSON'S PARENTS DIED... AND GAVE THE WORLD ROBIN.
AND POOR *JASON*... HIS PARENTS, TOO.

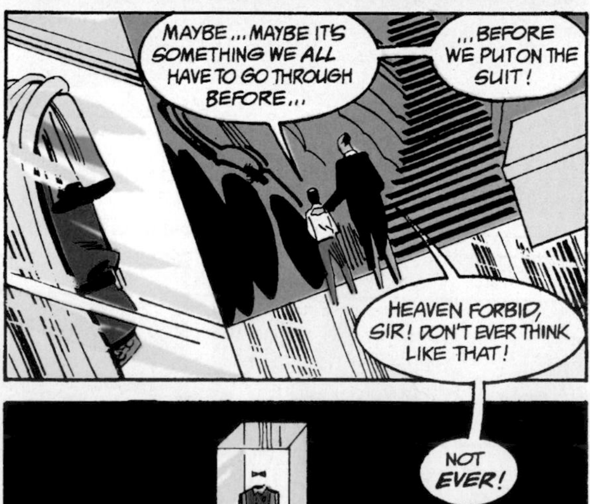
MAYBE... MAYBE IT'S SOMETHING WE *ALL* HAVE TO GO THROUGH BEFORE...
...BEFORE WE PUT ON THE SUIT!
HEAVEN FORBID, SIR! DON'T EVER THINK LIKE THAT!

NOT *EVER!*
NEXT ISSUE:
FIRE WALK!

BATMAN IN

Detective COMICS

APPROVED BY THE COMICS CODE AUTHORITY

GRANT
BREYFOGLE
MITCHELL

Cover art by Norm Breyfogle

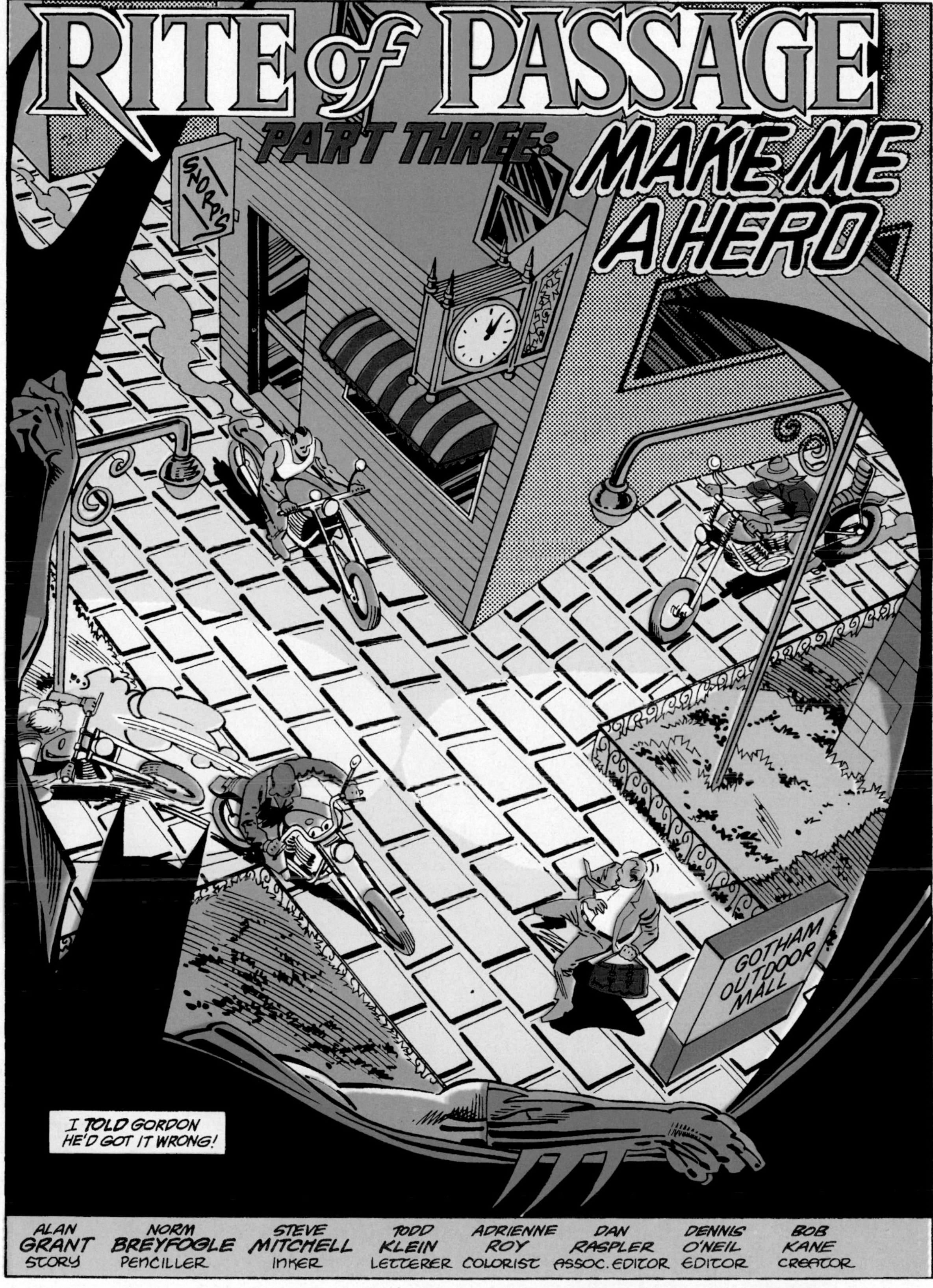

ALAN GRANT STORY · NORM BREYFOGLE PENCILLER · STEVE MITCHELL INKER · TODD KLEIN LETTERER · ADRIENNE ROY COLORIST · DAN RASPLER ASSOC. EDITOR · DENNIS O'NEIL EDITOR · BOB KANE CREATOR

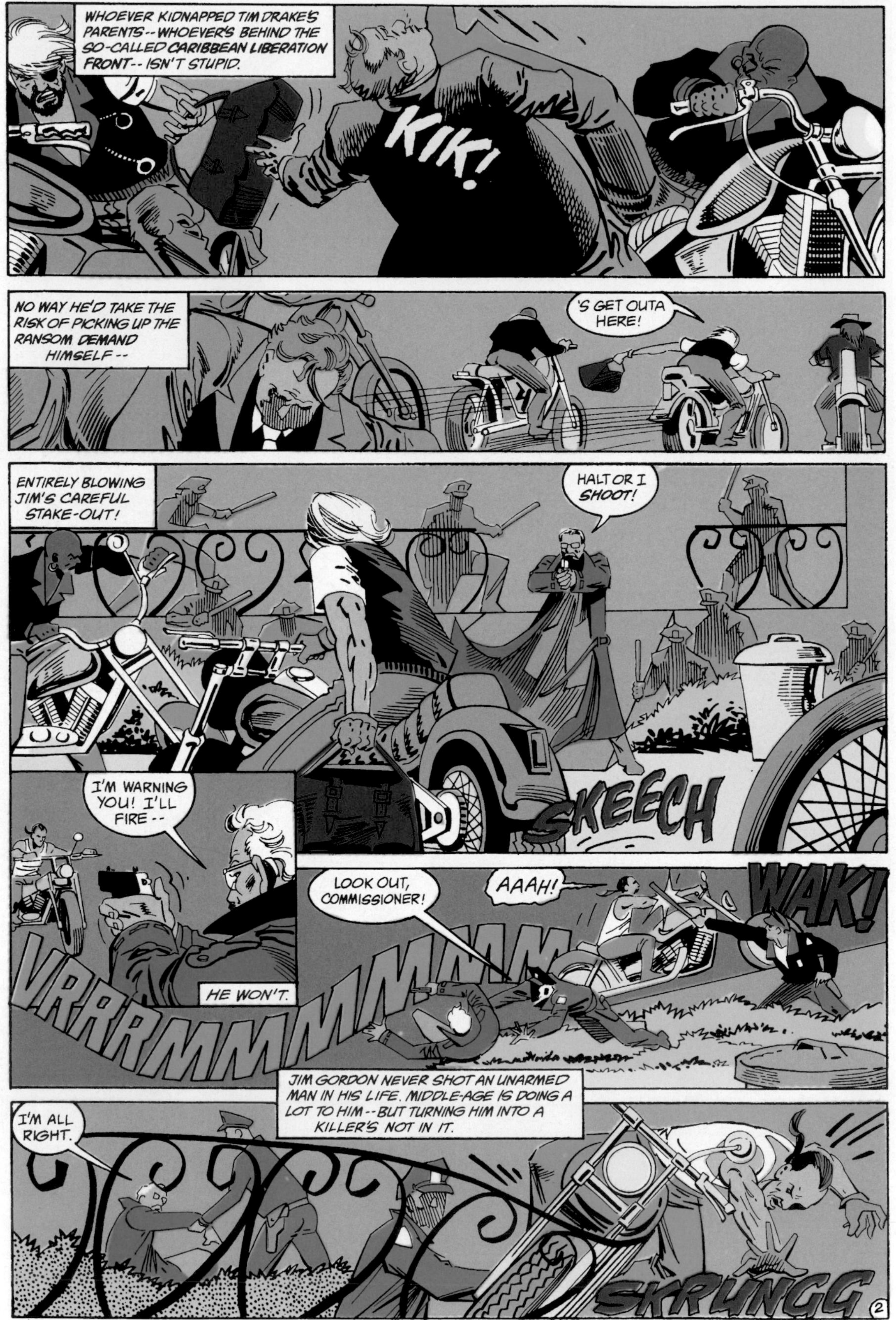
WHOEVER KIDNAPPED TIM DRAKE'S PARENTS--WHOEVER'S BEHIND THE SO-CALLED CARIBBEAN LIBERATION FRONT-- ISN'T STUPID.
KIK!
NO WAY HE'D TAKE THE RISK OF PICKING UP THE RANSOM DEMAND HIMSELF--
'S GET OUTA HERE!
ENTIRELY BLOWING JIM'S CAREFUL STAKE-OUT!
HALT OR I SHOOT!
SKEECH
I'M WARNING YOU! I'LL FIRE--
HE WON'T.
VRRRMMMMMMMM
LOOK OUT, COMMISSIONER!
AAAH!
WAK!
JIM GORDON NEVER SHOT AN UNARMED MAN IN HIS LIFE. MIDDLE-AGE IS DOING A LOT TO HIM--BUT TURNING HIM INTO A KILLER'S NOT IN IT.
I'M ALL RIGHT.
SKRUNGG

VRMMM
NEVER MIND ME! IF THEY GET AWAY, WE DON'T HAVE A SINGLE LEAD!

THERE ARE TWENTY COPS DOWN THERE. THEY DON'T NEED ME.
THAT'S FAR ENOUGH, CREEP--!

FWAK!
AGH!

GOTHAM
MALL
HE'S GETTING AWAY WITH THE MONEY!
VRRMMMMMMMM

BLAM
BLAM

SORRY, COMMISSIONER-- WE GOT THE OTHERS, BUT THE ONE WITH THE SATCHEL ...
WHAT A FOUL UP!

WHY DOES HE ALWAYS HAVE TO BE RIGHT?
YOU'RE GETTING TOO OLD, JIM. TOO OLD FOR MIDNIGHT CHASES-- BIKE GANGS--

TOO OLD TO RUN WITH THE WARRIORS.

YOUR FRIENDS...?
COPS GOT 'EM. MEANS I GOTTA FIND BAIL.

PRICE IS UP. SAME AGAIN.
YOU DESERVE IT, MY FRIEND.

WHAT THE HE--?
SHNG
HERE--
SHRIP

GAA--
GAK! GAK!

BELLADONNA. JIMSON ROOT, MAYBE. HE WAS DEAD FROM THE MOMENT THAT NEEDLE BROKE SKIN, HEART AND NERVOUS SYSTEM EXPLODING IN SPASM.

FURY FILLS ME.
A MAN HAS JUST BEEN MURDERED BEFORE MY EYES. ON MY STREETS! NOT MUCH OF A MAN, MAYBE--BUT EVEN HE DESERVED BETTER.
FOR AN INSTANT, I ALMOST FORGET--

TIM'S PARENTS.
SHK

I'M PRETTY SURE I KNOW WHERE HE'S GOING. BUT I HAVE TO BE **POSITIVE**.

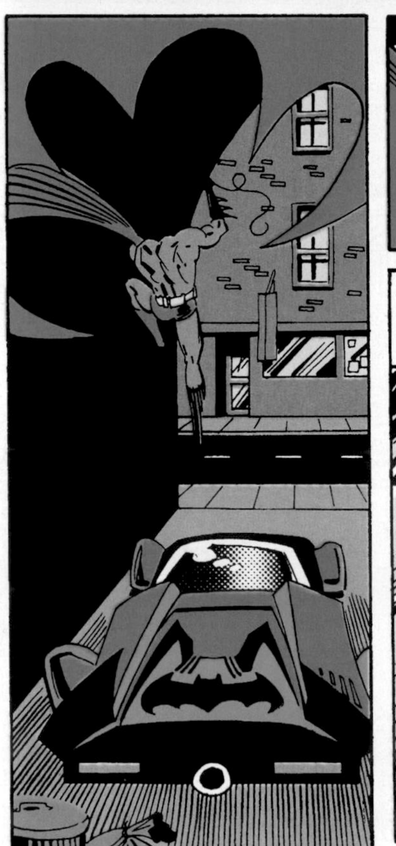

HE'S NOT HANGING AROUND TO CATCH THE SIGHTS. HEADED DIRECTLY FOR THE AIRPORT!

LUCKY I KEEP A PASSPORT IN THE CAR. TIM WILL NEVER FORGIVE ME IF I GET THIS ONE WRONG.
I'LL NEVER FORGIVE MYSELF.

SKREE SKREE
IN THE NAME OF PAPA LEGBA!
IN THE NAMES OF BARON SAMEDI-- MAITRE CARREFOUR-- OGOUN--WANGOL-- DANGER MINA!

BY THE POWERS OF THE ZANGES--LET THIS MAN BE TROUBLED NO MORE BY DARK SPIRITS!

GO NOW INTO A FITTING HOME! GO! GO!
GUUH! GUH! GGGGUGH!

I TELL YOU-- TROUBLE HIM NO MORE!

SKEE
SHUK

--NO GOOD! I CAN'T EVEN BUDGE THEM!

WHAT-- WHAT ARE THEY DOING OUT THERE?
MORE OF THEIR SUPERSTITIOUS BLOODY RITUALS! KILLING SOMETHING ELSE, NO DOUBT!

THEY WERE TALKING EARLIER--ABOUT SOME CEREMONY THEY'RE HOLDING TOMORROW NIGHT. THEY--THEY SEEM TO EXPECT THE RANSOM TO BE PAID BY THEN.
I HOPE SO. THEY MURDERED JEREMY WITHOUT BLINKING AN EYE. NO REASON THEY SHOULD BALK AT US!

I... I'VE NEVER BEEN SO SCARED IN MY LIFE!
ME NEITHER. BUT WE HAVE TO BE STRONG, JANET!
THINK OF TIM--HOW HE MUST BE FEELING. POOR KID MUST BE WORRIED SICK!

IF ONLY... IF ONLY YOU KNEW WHAT LIFE HAD COMING, YOU WOULDN'T EVER WASTE ANY OF THE GOOD THINGS!

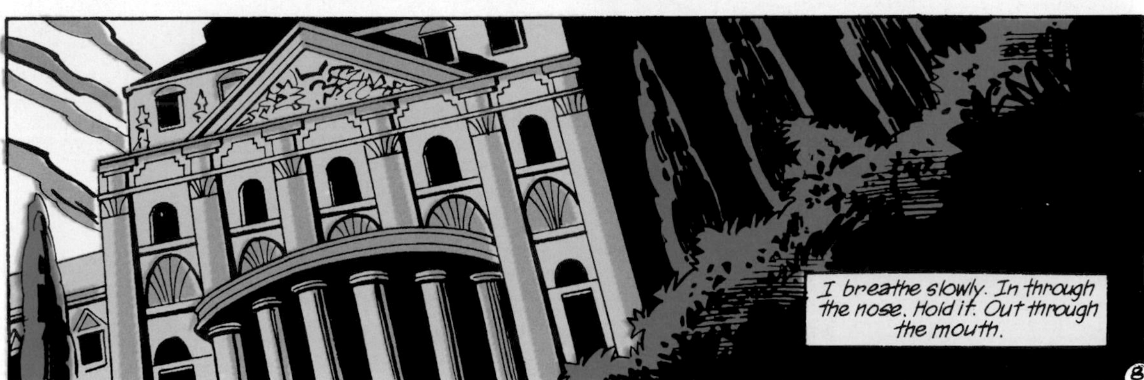
I breathe slowly. In through the nose. Hold it. Out through the mouth.

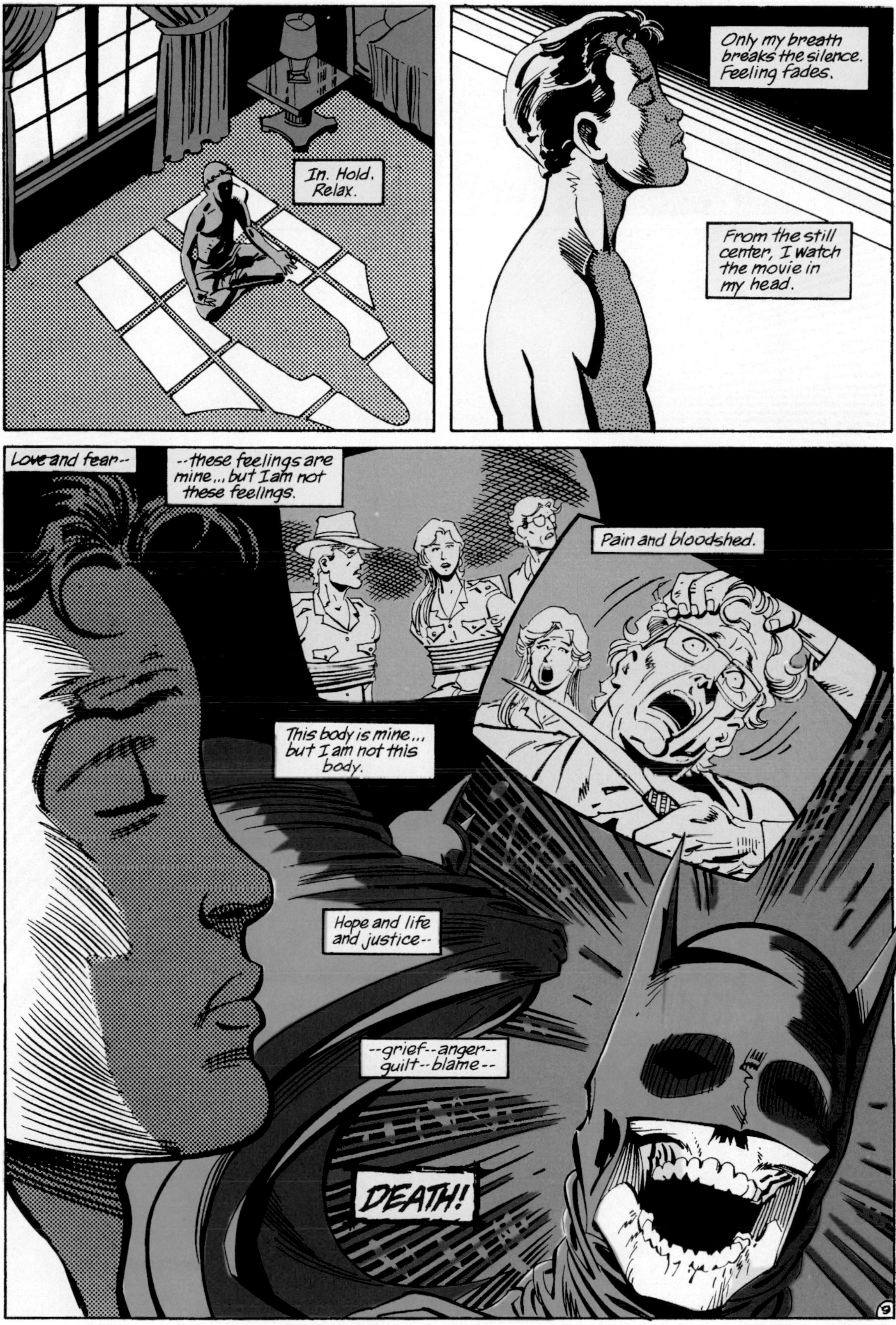

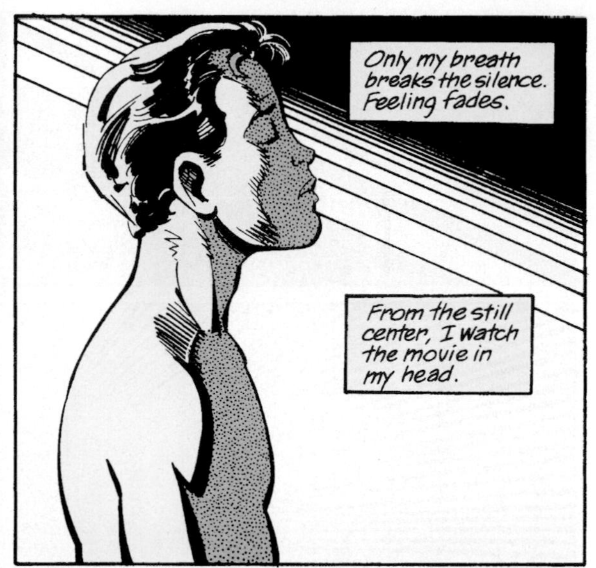

Love and fear--

--these feelings are mine... but I am not these feelings.

Pain and bloodshed.

This body is mine... but I am not this body.

Hope and life and justice--

--grief--anger--guilt--blame--

DEATH!

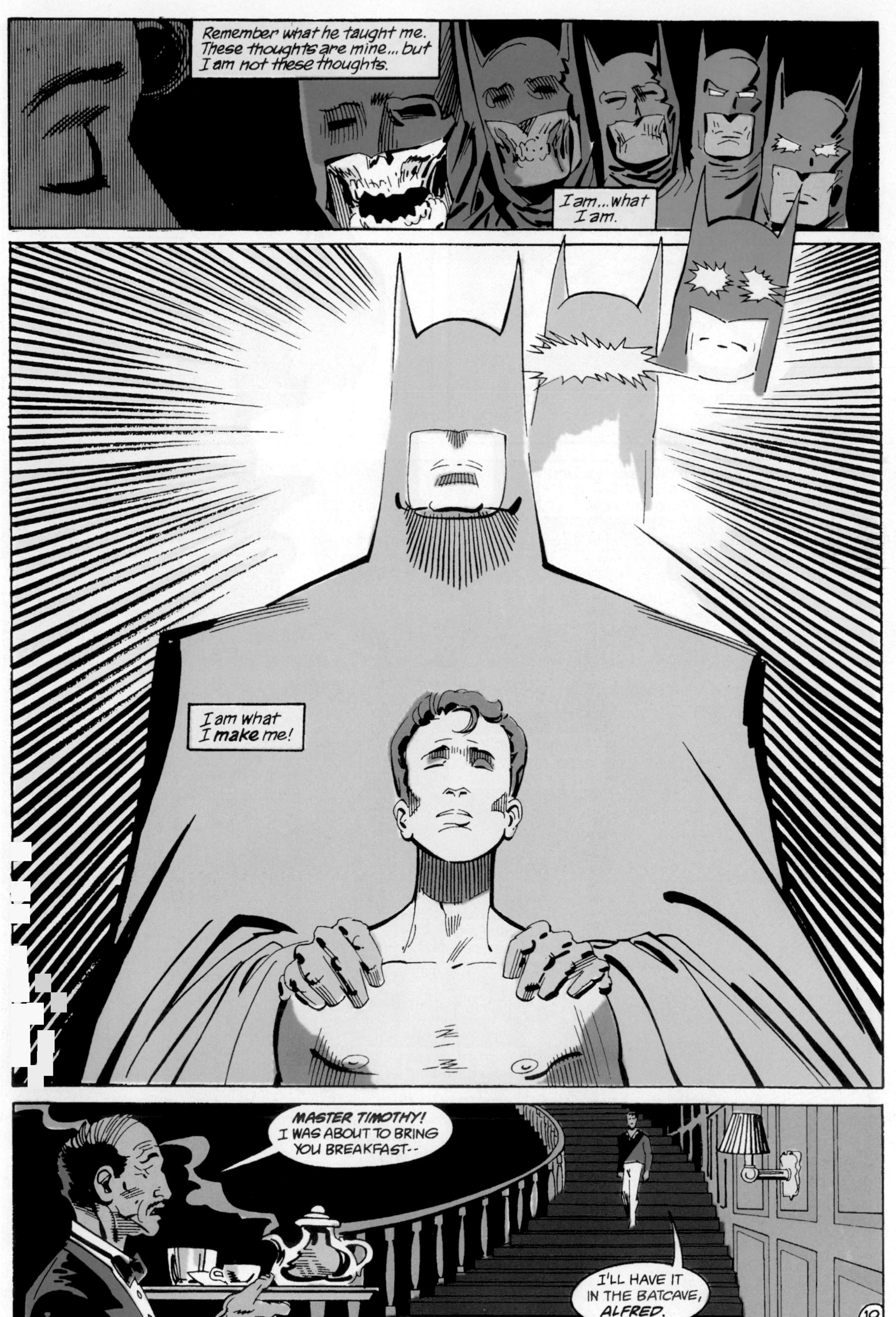
Remember what he taught me. These thoughts are mine... but I am not these thoughts.
I am...what I am.
I am what I **make** me!
MASTER TIMOTHY! I WAS ABOUT TO BRING YOU BREAKFAST--
I'LL HAVE IT IN THE BATCAVE, **ALFRED**.

BRUCE--?
DIDN'T COME HOME LAST NIGHT. DIDN'T CALL TO SAY WHY NOT.

ARE YOU WORRIED?
I LEARNED LONG SINCE, MASTER TIMOTHY, THAT ALL THE WORRY IN THE WORLD DOESN'T CHANGE A THING! SO...I DON'T.

THAT'S WHAT I'VE FIGURED. IF I'VE ENERGY TO BURN, I MIGHT AS WELL CHANNEL IT INTO GOOD USE!

SOMEWHERE OUT THERE IN COMPUTERLAND THERE'S A GUY STEALING MILLIONS OF DOLLARS. I'M GOING TO FIND HIM!
TAK TAK TAK TAK
BYE-BYE DODO LOVE, THE MONEYSPIDER XXXX

NO POINT WAITING FOR HIM TO STRIKE AGAIN. TIME I TOOK THE GAME TO HIM!
IT'S A JOY TO HEAR YOU SPEAK SO POSITIVELY, SIR. I WAS BEGINNING TO WONDER IF--

HEY--IF THE HEROES CAN'T DO THEIR JOB...WHO CAN?

YOU HAD ME ANXIOUS FOR A WHILE THERE. BUT YOU ARE A DETERMINED YOUNG MAN.
NOW ALL I HAVE TO WORRY ABOUT IS MASTER BRUCE!

YOU ARE GOING OUT AGAIN, FATHER?

SINCE YOU MET THAT OBEAH MAN, YOU ARE HARDLY EVER HOME!
NOT FOR MUCH LONGER, BOY. GREAT THINGS ARE COMING OUR WAY!

AFTER TONIGHT WE WILL BE RICH--ABLE TO GET OUT OF THIS STINKING HOLE-- TO DO WHAT WE PLEASE!
RICH? BUT HOW?
THANK THE OBEAH MAN, BOY--

--AND MY BAKA!
PAT PAT

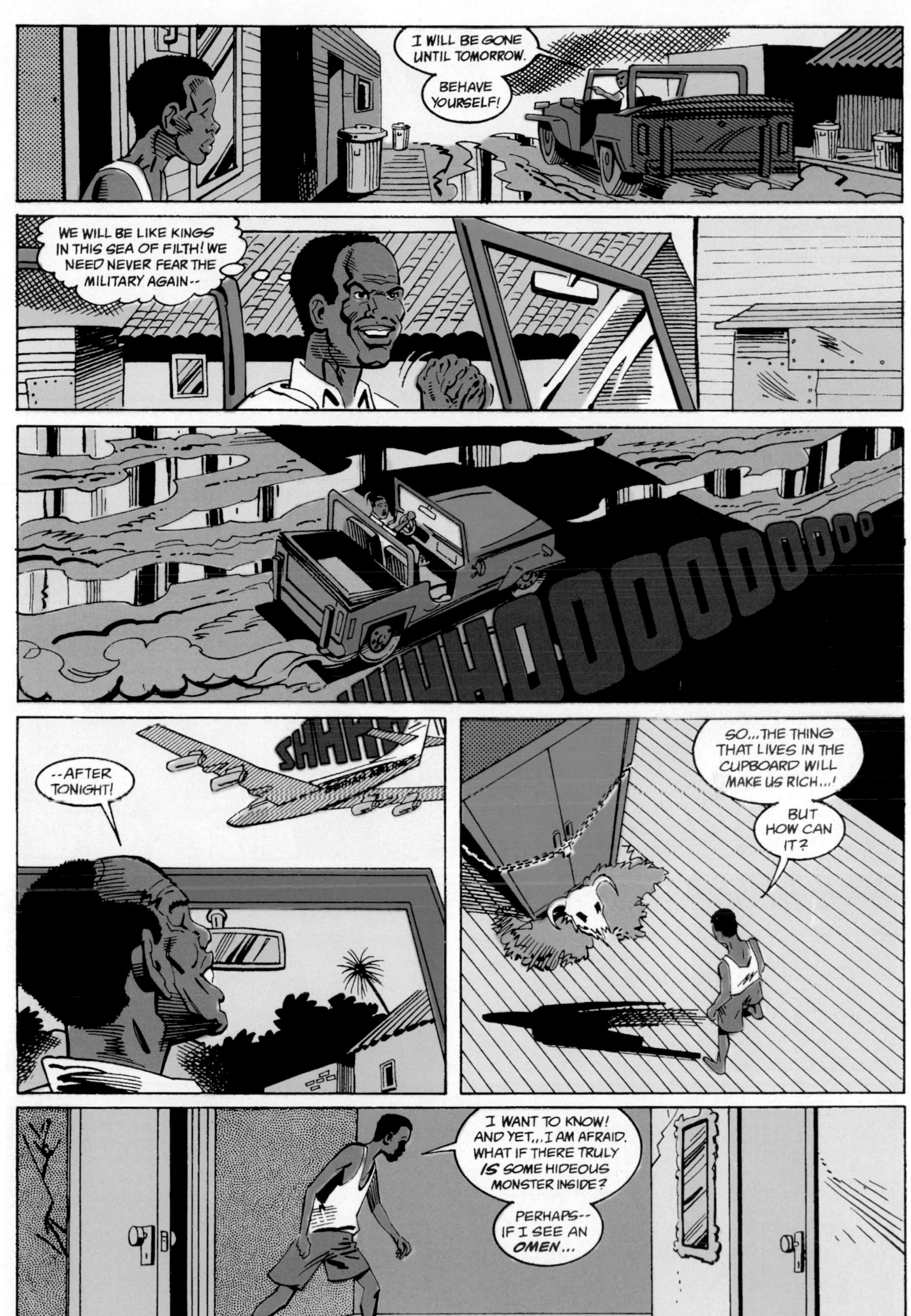
I WILL BE GONE UNTIL TOMORROW.
BEHAVE YOURSELF!
WE WILL BE LIKE KINGS IN THIS SEA OF FILTH! WE NEED NEVER FEAR THE MILITARY AGAIN--
WHHOOOOOOOOOOOO
SHHHH
--AFTER TONIGHT!
SO... THE THING THAT LIVES IN THE CUPBOARD WILL MAKE US RICH...!
BUT HOW CAN IT?
I WANT TO KNOW! AND YET... I AM AFRAID. WHAT IF THERE TRULY *IS* SOME HIDEOUS MONSTER INSIDE?
PERHAPS-- IF I SEE AN ***OMEN***...

HAITI LIVES IN A HAZE OF FEAR AND POVERTY.
GOTHAM AIRLINES
SECOND POOREST COUNTRY IN THE WORLD, RIGHT ON OUR BACK DOORSTEP. HOW DO WE LET IT HAPPEN?
FIFTY BUCKS. AND TEN MILLION IN BEARER BONDS WALK IN UN-INSPECTED.
LET ME SEE YOUR BAG, MONSIEUR!
IS THIS WHAT YOU'RE LOOKING FOR?
SAME PRICE FOR A BAT SUIT!

ANOMALY! BANK OF CAMBODIA ACCT. #'S
34Z N106 TR2045
X74 NCC30 115R3
89F 1106 CAM
CC25 1010 XYMG1
MTVX 4789 CCB
LL NTR3 XZQ R6

VERY INTERESTING! THE DAY AFTER THIS ***MONEYSPIDER*** STOLE THE MILLION FROM ***WAYNETECH,*** ALMOST A THOUSAND PEASANT FARMERS IN ***CAMBODIA*** WERE GIVEN BANK ACCOUNTS, AND CREDITED WITH A THOUSAND DOLLARS EACH!

IF THAT'S ***COINCIDENCE,*** MY NAME'S ***DUCK!***

SO... OUR MONEYSPIDER HAS A ***CONSCIENCE.*** OPENS UP A WHOLE NEW FIELD OF PLACES TO LOOK...

I feel like I'm still meditating.
Life's out there, but I'm removed, detached, at the center of an electronic web reaching across the world--
Probing--analyzing--scanning--flicking from country to country at the touch of a plastic key--
--following a trail that I know with growing certainty is going to lead me exactly where I want to go.
GOTCHA!
555-6729
R

ER... ARE YOU SURE ABOUT THIS, YOUNG MAN?
GOTHAM JUVENILE CORRECTION HALL

I'M AFRAID I CAN'T TELL YOU HOW I KNOW, MR. WALLACE-- BUT I'M POSITIVE.
EVEN APART FROM ANYTHING ELSE, HE ONLY HAS A LAP-TOP, FOR GOODNESS' SAKE!

TELEPHONES
OUT OF ORDER
HE DOESN'T HAVE A MODEM-- AND IF HE DID, THERE'S NOWHERE TO CONNECT IT! THESE ARE THE ONLY TELEPHONES--

OUT OF ORDER
OH.
THIS IS HIS ROOM--

POLITICAL SCIENCE
ILLUMINATUS
GOOD AFTERNOON, "MONEYSPIDER"--
OR DO YOU PREFER ANARKY?

ANARCHY
THE ANARCHISTS J. JOLL
APOSTLES OF REVOLUTION
NOMAD
PROUDON
BAKUNIN
IMAGINE
LONNIE, SOME RATHER SERIOUS ACCUSATIONS ARE BEING MADE ABOUT YOU. IT'S SUGGESTED YOU--
SIPHONED OFF BETTER THAN TEN MILLION BUCKS FROM CORPORATE ACCOUNTS AND REDISTRIBUTED IT TO THIRD WORLD COUNTRIES?

SURE. IT WAS ME. EASY ONCE YOU KNOW WHAT YOU'RE DOING!
SO WHAT YOU GONNA DO? MAKE ME PAY IT BACK?

LONNIE, YOUR ATTITUDE IS GOING TO LAND YOU IN REAL TROUBLE! YOUR AIMS MAY BE COMMENDABLE--BUT YOU MUST SEE THAT YOUR MEANS ARE WRONG!
YOU GAVE AWAY MONEY THAT YOU YOURSELF STOLE!
THE WEST'S BEEN STEALING FROM THEM FOR YEARS! I'M ONLY REDRESSING THE BALANCE A LITTLE!
BLACK FLA
POLL TAX OFFIC BOMBED
BATMAN VERSU ANARKY!!

I'VE DONE A LITTLE READING ABOUT ANARCHY MYSELF, LONNIE. I WOULDN'T MIND DISCUSSING IT WITH YOU. I MEAN, MY UNDERSTANDING IS--
V FOR VENDETTA

DISCUSS IT WITH THE HEADMASTER, WISE-GUY!
I should have known. The essence of anarchy is surprise--

THERE'S NOWHERE TO RUN, LONNIE!

His HEART might be in the RIGHT place--but he has all the makings of a BAD guy, just the same!

If you're going to take them out, Batman said--

OOFFF!

I'LL LEAVE IT IN YOUR HANDS, THEN, MR. WALLACE...?
ER, I SUPPOSE SO, MR.--ER, MR....
OH, JUST CALL ME A CONCERNED PASSER-BY!

CAPITALIST SCUM! RUNNING DOG LACKEY OF THE IMPERIALIST WARMONGERS!
THE PEOPLE KNOW YOUR FACE! WE WON'T FORGET!

WHEN THE REVOLUTION COMES, YOU'RE FIRST ON THE LIST!

I DID it!
I figured it out and tracked him down. I CAUGHT him!

And I hardly once allowed myself to think about... painful things.
I just wish Bruce were here.

I want to tell him--
B-B-BRUCE!

I...
I HAVE BAD NEWS.
NEXT ISSUE:
TRIAL BY FIRE!

DC
621
US $1.00
CAN $1.25
SEP 90
BATMAN IN
Detective
COMICS
APPROVED BY THE COMICS CODE AUTHORITY
GRANT
BREYFOGLE
MITCHELL

Cover art by Norm Breyfogle

ALAN GRANT Script
NORM BREYFOGLE Penciller
STEVE MITCHELL Inker
ADRIENNE ROY Colors
TODD KLEIN Letters
DAN RASPLER Assoc. Editor
DENNIS O'NEIL Editor
BATMAN Created by BOB KANE

YOUR PARENTS' COMPANY HAD DECIDED TO PAY THE KIDNAP RANSOM. I MANAGED TO TAIL THE PICK-UP MAN.
AS I SUSPECTED, HE WAS ON THE FIRST PLANE OUT OF GOTHAM FOR HAITI!!
"BRUCE WAYNE WAS ON THE SAME FLIGHT--"
Uhh... FOLLOW THAT JEEP!
CURRENCY EXCHANGE
I STOP ALSO, M'SIEUR?
NO!
ROUND THE CORNER, PLEASE.
THIS IS NOT SUCH A GOOD PLACE FOR YOU, M'SIEUR. NO HOTEL, HUNGRY PEOPLE...
I'LL BE ALL RIGHT, THANKS. I HAVE... Uhh, A FRIEND.
"THE STREET WAS EMPTY, THOUGH I KNEW I'D BEEN SEEN. MEN IN SUITS RATE THE SAME AS MEN IN UNIFORM TO THESE PEOPLE!"

"I HAD NO PLAN, NO LEADS. I CONSIDERED GOING IN AND TACKLING THEM HEAD ON-- BUT WHAT IF THERE WAS AN 'ALL SAFE' SIGNAL THEY HAD TO GIVE?

"BETTER TO BIDE MY TIME. SOONER OR LATER, THE MONEY AND YOUR PARENTS WERE BOUND TO CROSS PATHS."

TO MONEY! TO POWER!

TNK

TO THE *OBEAH MAN!*

MONEY!
COME ON!

I... I CAN'T STAND IT, JACK--!
YOU--OBEAH MAN, OR WHATEVER YOU CALL YOURSELF! MY WIFE NEEDS WATER!
THAT IS UNFORTUNATE, MR. DRAKE--
--FOR SHE MAY NOT HAVE ANY! NOT QUITE YET, ANYWAY. BUT SOON, SHE WILL DRINK ALL SHE WILL EVER WANT.
SPSH
YOU SADISTIC BRUTE! IF I EVER--
OBEAH MAN!
LOUIS AND MALICIEN!
THE MONEY--!
ALL WENT WELL?
LIKE TAKING BLOOD FROM A WOUND!
THERE--YOU HAVE YOUR FILTHY RANSOM! NOW KEEP YOUR PART OF THE BARGAIN--SET US FREE! LET US OUT OF HERE!
5

I FEAR THERE HAS BEEN A MISUNDERSTANDING, MR. DRAKE. IT IS YOUR SOULS WHICH WILL BE FREED.
RANSOM OR NO, YOU ARE GOING TO DIE!
THIRTEEN OF THEM. TWO WITH GUNS, MOST OF THE OTHERS ARMED. I HAVE TO GET THIS RIGHT THE FIRST TIME!
THE MOON IS FULL--THE COALS BURN HOT! ALL AROUND, THE INVISIBLE FIRE LOAS WRITHE AND CURL!
IN THE NAMES OF BARON SAMEDI, PAPA LEGBA, WE BESEECH THEM--

ACCEPT THE SACRIFICE WE OFFER! IN TURN, GIVE US WHAT WE SEEK--
POWER!
JOIN ME! DO NOT BE AFRAID!
BELIEVE! BELIEVE!

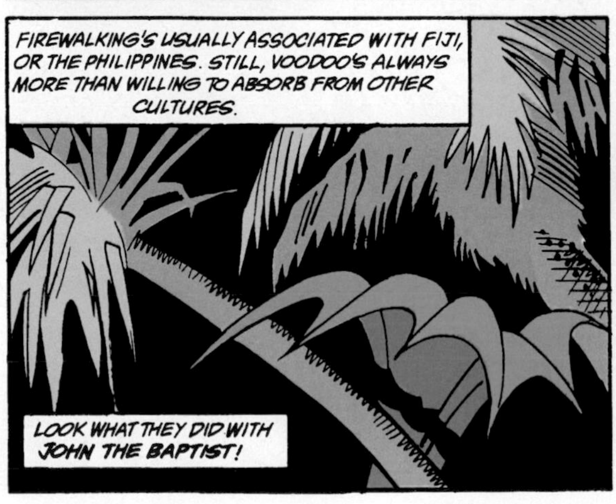

PERSPIRATION FORMS A BARRIER BETWEEN THE COALS AND THE SKIN-- SOMEONE PROPERLY TRAINED CAN STAND ON IT FOR A SHORT TIME.
LET'S SEE HOW IT DOES WITH BOOTS!
MALICIEN-- LOUIS! DO IT!
BELIEVE!
BAKA, BE WITH ME! BAKA, LEND ME STRENGTH!
WHAT--?
THE GUNS FIRST!
SHOK
SHAK
AN EVIL SPIRIT!

NO SPIRIT! HE IS A MAN!
STOP HIM--!
BLAM!
P-POW
WUMP
I--I DON'T BELIEVE IT! BATMAN!
IF I CAN TAKE HIM OUT, THE OTHERS SHOULD BE EASY! CREEP'S GOT NO GLASS JAW, THOUGH--
SOK!
SNAG
GAK..?
TUK

I DO NOT KNOW WHY YOU INTERFERE, OUTSIDER--

--BUT THE LOAS WILL CLAIM A *THIRD SOUL* THIS NIGHT!
BATMAN! BEHIND YOU--!

WAK
YOU COME FOR *THEM?*
SLASH

KILL HIM!
HEAT'S GETTING TOO MUCH! CAN'T TAKE ANY LONGER OVER THIS--
10

WAK
AARGH!
NO--
NO!
AIEEEE!
AAAH!
AIYYY!
ANOTHER COUPLE OF SECONDS--
SLASH
OH, THANK GOD! THANK GOD!

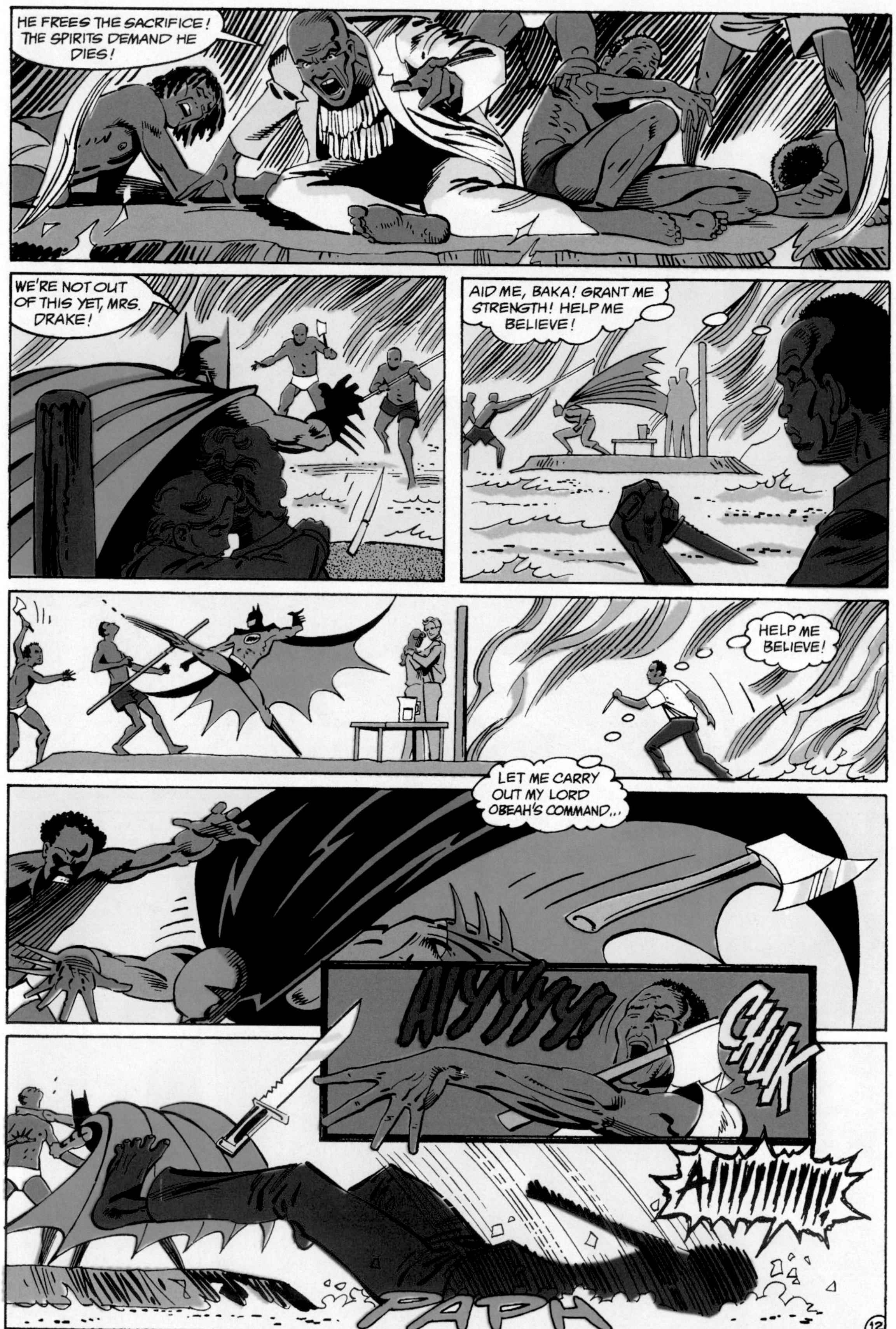
HE FREES THE SACRIFICE! THE SPIRITS DEMAND HE DIES!
WE'RE NOT OUT OF THIS YET, MRS. DRAKE!
AID ME, BAKA! GRANT ME STRENGTH! HELP ME BELIEVE!
HELP ME BELIEVE!
LET ME CARRY OUT MY LORD OBEAH'S COMMAND...
AIYYYY!
CHUK
AIIIIIIIII!
PAPH

OH, MY GOD!
AIEEEEEEEEEEEEEE...

I THINK I'M GOING TO BE SICK--!
HERE-- DRINK THIS!

WE'RE GOING TO HAVE TO MAKE A BREAK FOR IT. ARE YOU TWO UP TO IT?
WE CAN TRY, BATMAN!

JUST GIVE ME A MOMENT--
URHH!

THE WATER--!
GULKK!

GULK!
SPSSHH

POISON!
FOOL! YOUR HEROICS WERE ALL IN VAIN!
THEY WERE FATED TO DIE!
RRRRRRRRRRRRRRR

RRRAAAAAGHHHHH!
I'VE FAILED.
I'VE FAILED!

"I PUT THEM IN THE JEEP, DROVE DIRECT TO THE HOSPITAL IN TOWN. THERE WAS NOTHING THEY COULD DO.
"JIMSON ROOT EXTRACT. IT'S A NERVE TOXIN.
"I HAD TO INFORM THE AUTHORITIES. THEN I WAS ABLE TO CHARTER A FLIGHT BACK TO GOTHAM."
I'M SORRY, TIM. TRULY SORRY.
DOCTOR...!
HOW IS HE? IS THERE ANY CHANCE...?
NOT MUCH.
HIS CENTRAL NERVOUS SYSTEM'S BADLY DAMAGED.

HE'S PARALYZED.
I KNOW HOW YOU MUST FEEL.
DO YOU?

YES.

I KNOW. I'M SORRY.

For a moment I relax against him. I feel his strength, flowing into me from those bottomless reserves.

He absorbs my fear, takes it all on his own shoulders.
Hero's shoulders.

And then--
--I stare into the DARK SIDE.

The night-demon's cowl...
...the cape like some jagged, evil stain... spreading, swirling around me...
...sucking me into a lifetime in hell!
TIMOTHY...?
19

YOU CAN GO IN FOR A FEW MINUTES, IF YOU LIKE. BE GENTLE. HE CAN HEAR YOU, BUT... HE CAN'T RESPOND.

DO YOU WANT ME...?
NO.

DAD...

DAD... MOM'S DEAD.
AND YOU...

OH DAD...
I'M SO AFRAID!

THE WORLD IS ROTTEN.
THERE'S NO FAIRNESS-- NO JUSTICE. NO SENSE.

HOW DO YOU MAKE UP FOR WHAT HE'S LOST? HOW DO YOU PAY BACK THE PAIN, AND THE FEAR, AND THE LONELY YEARS?

DRAW POWER FROM DEATH? BECOME LIKE ME? THE NIGHT-MONSTER. THE MAN WHO TAINTS THE LIVES OF ALL AROUND HIM.
IS THAT WHAT I WANT FOR HIM?

IS THAT WHAT HE'LL WANT FOR HIMSELF?

--MONEY! THAT WAS THE SECRET POWER!

AT LEAST, IT WAS IN THE CASE!
WHAT ABOUT THE BAKA? WAS THAT MONEY, TOO?
I FIGURED IT WOULD BE...
"...SO I WAITED TILL DAD AND HIS FRIEND LEFT, THEN PLUCKED UP MY COURAGE AND BURST OPEN THE DOOR...
"BUT IT WASN'T MONEY--"
A BALL OF MUD--AND FEATHERS--AND BONES!

"ALL THESE NIGHT-MARES--SHIVERING EVERY TIME I PASSED IT--AND ALL FOR A BALL OF MUD!"

I WAS JUST SO ANNOYED! DAD'LL BEAT ME STUPID! HE TOLD ME A HUNDRED TIMES TO KEEP AWAY!
I WONDER WHERE HE IS, ANYWAY? HE'S USUALLY HOME BY NOW...
TNK

THE END

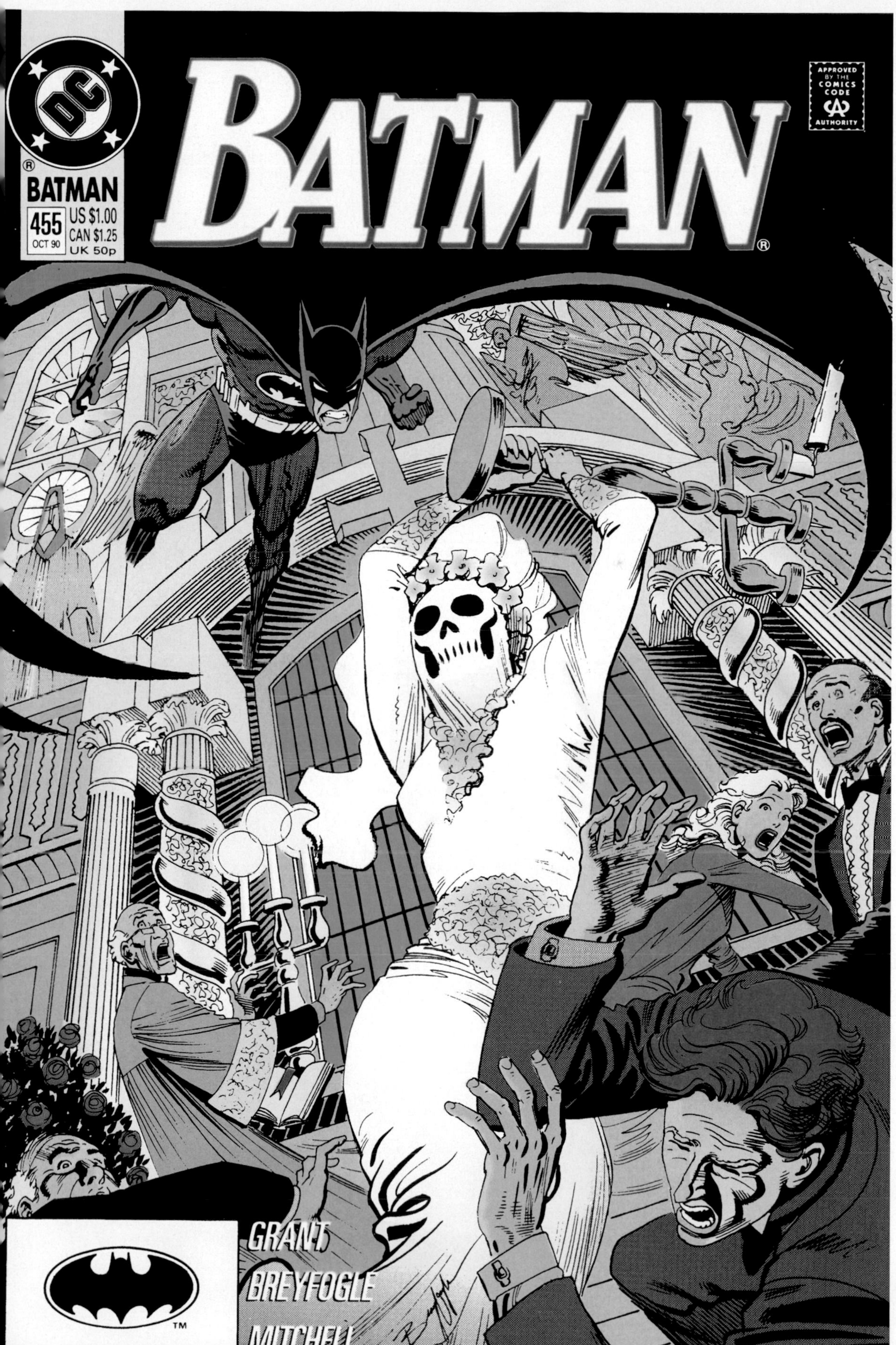

BATMAN
455
OCT 90
US $1.00
CAN $1.25
UK 50p
APPROVED BY THE COMICS CODE AUTHORITY
BATMAN
GRANT
BREYFOGLE
MITCHELL

Cover art by Norm Breyfogle

ALAN GRANT WRITER · NORM BREYFOGLE PENCILLER · STEVE MITCHELL INKER · ADRIENNE ROY COLORIST · TODD KLEIN LETTERER · KELLEY PUCKETT ASST. EDITOR · DENNIS O'NEIL EDITOR · BOB KANE CREATOR · KEVIN BREYFOGLE ART ASSIST

ALMOST DAWN. ANOTHER NIGHT SAFELY CHARTED.
THE CITY STAYS THE SAME. ONLY I GET OLDER.
THE BLOOD IS DRYING ON THE STREETS. HOSPITAL CASUALTY CREWS RELAX. THE NIGHT-PEOPLE DRINK UP AND HEAD HOME.
BUS STOP
BAR
EVIL SLINKS BACK INTO ITS HOLES, AFRAID TO FACE THE COMING OF THE LIGHT.
BUS STOP
ALTHOUGH--
BLAM
--NOT ALWAYS!
BLAM
BLAM
BLAM

FOUR SHOTS FIRED. AT LEAST TWO LEFT. COULD HAVE ANOTHER GUN.

SMASH!

KRAK!

TAKE NO CHANCES.

I SAID AMBULANCE!
Y-YESSIR!

BADADIDDLADATDADIDDLADATDA DA DAAAA DA DIDDLA

KLIK

EVERYBODY UP!
MOVE IT, FOZZY! YOU'RE ON BREAKFAST!
DONK!
...H-HUH? OWW!

THIS IS RIDIC, LEGS! WE AIN'T GOT NO REASON FOR WAKIN' UP. IT'S STILL DARK--
DISCIPLINE, THAT'S YER REASON, BEEKER. Y'GOTTA HAVE DISCIPLINE, OR THE WHOLE SCHMOOZLE JUST FALLS T' PIECES--
--AN' THEN WHERE WOULD WE BE?

WHERE ARE WE NOW, FER PETE'S SAKE? LIKE, WHO WANTS TA WAKE UP TA THIS?

KLIK

HEY! WHAT'S THE BIG IDEA? THINK THIS IS A ZOO?
GET OUTA HERE!

LOUSY TOURIST!
I'M SORRY. I DIDN'T MEAN TO OFFEND ANYONE. IF...IF IT BOTHERS YOU THIS MUCH, I'LL DESTROY THE FILM.

AHH, 'S OKAY, LADY. I'M JUST CRUSTY FIRST THING IN THE MORNIN'!
YEAH-- ALL THE REST O' THE TIME, TOO!
TAKE A LOAD OFF. WHATCHA UP TO, ANYWAY?

MY NAME IS VICKI VALE. I'M A PHOTO-JOURNALIST. I'M DOING A PIECE ON THE HOMELESS FOR GOTHAM VIEW. IT'S ABOUT TIME FOLKS KNEW THE FACTS ABOUT THIS CITY!
YA COME TO THE RIGHT PLACE, HONEY!
FOZZY! EXTRA PORTION FOR OUR GUEST HERE!

NO--REALLY. I NEVER EAT BEFORE LUNCH.
G'WAN! YOU'LL LIKE IT. MEAT. PROTEIN. GOTTA KEEP YOUR STRENGTH UP.

ER...WHAT IS IT, EXACTLY?
SNF

RAT.

EXCUSE ME.
HAW HAW! DIDJA SEE HER FACE? WOTTA PICTURE!
RAT? YOU KILL ME, LEGS!
WHY DIDN'T YA JUST TELL HER THE TRUTH-- YA DON'T KNOW WHAT IT IS, 'CAUSE IT CAME OUT O' THE HOTEL TRASH!
LOUSY TOURIST!
AEIEEEEEEEE
--TUNATELY, THE TRASH CUSHIONED THE IMPACT. SHE'LL BE A MASS OF BRUISES, BUT OTHERWISE ALL RIGHT.
BUS STOP
HOW--HOW DID I DO..?
DO? YOU KILLED TWO PEOPLE--WOUNDED TWO OTHERS!
THAT'S...NOT BAD. I'M SIXTY-SEVEN, YOU KNOW. I'VE NEVER COMMITTED A CRIME BEFORE!
BUT WHY, FOR GOD'S SAKE? WHAT MADE YOU DO IT?
6

I... I DON'T KNOW. CALL IT...
CALL IT AN OLD LADY'S WHIM!
YOU COULDN'T HAVE KNOWN, BATMAN. DON'T BLAME YOURSELF.
I DON'T.
I DIDN'T SHOOT ANYONE!
AMBU
MY MUMMY'S DEAD.
MY MUMMY'S DEAD.
PARENTS OF DICK GRAYSON MURDERED!
MOTHER OF JASON TODD MURDERED!
I CAN'T GET IT THROUGH MY HEAD...

RIP
JANET DRAKE
MURDERED!
NO! SHE CAN'T BE DEAD! IT ISN'T FAIR!
LIFE ISN'T FAIR.
DEATH ISN'T FAIR.
THAT'S NOT TRUE! IT HAS TO BE FAIR! IT HAS TO MEAN SOMETHING!
IT'S YOU WHO'S NOT FAIR! YOU'RE MONSTERS--HIDING UNDER MASKS!
TAKE THEM OFF!
LET ME SEE YOUR REAL FACES! I WANT TO KNOW WHAT YOU REALLY ARE!
8

WHAT ABOUT YOU? WHAT ARE YOU HIDING?
NO! NO!
I DON'T WANT TO SEE!
I'M AFRAID! I'M AFRAID--
TIM--
ARE YOU ALL RIGHT?
I WAS... DREAMING.
NIGHTMARE, I'D SAY. WANT TO TELL ME..?

NO! THAT IS--I'M OKAY NOW. IT WASN'T ANYTHING I CAN'T HANDLE.

BETTER GET UP. I... HATE TO REMIND YOU, BUT TODAY IS--
THE FUNERAL. HER FUNERAL.

MY MOMMY'S FUNERAL.

RAT?
HA! PIGEON, PROBABLY, OR THE REMAINS OF SOMEBODY'S BURGER! HE JUST SAID THAT TO SPOOK ME.
NO HARM IN LETTING HIM HAVE HIS LITTLE JOKE.

CAN'T BLAME HIM, REALLY. THE COST OF MY CAMERA ALONE WOULD FEED THEM ALL FOR A MONTH.
STILL, THE FEATURE WILL FOCUS INTEREST ON THEM--IF IT COMES OFF. SOME NICE SHOTS.

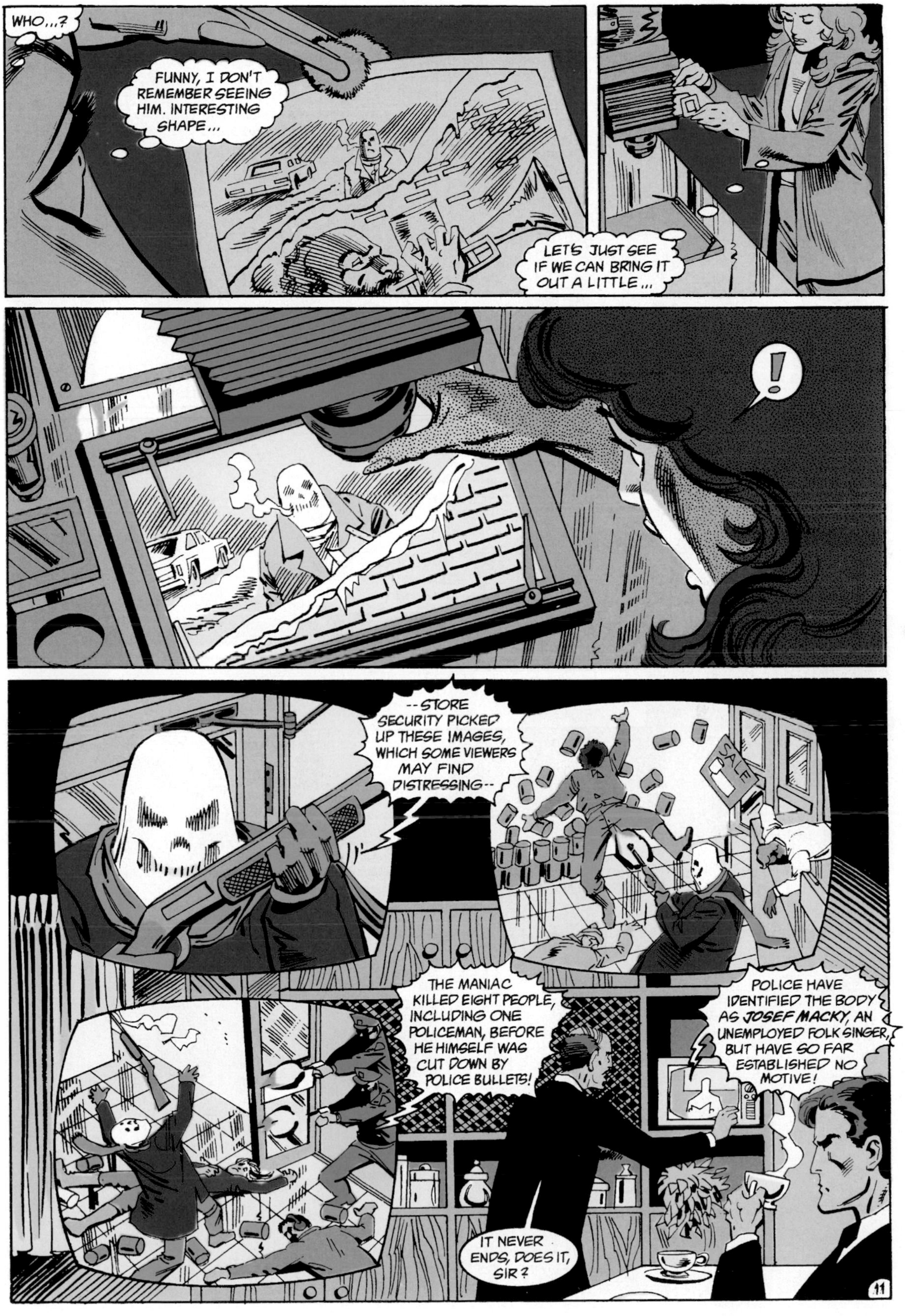

--STORE SECURITY PICKED UP THESE IMAGES, WHICH SOME VIEWERS MAY FIND DISTRESSING--

SALE

THE MANIAC KILLED EIGHT PEOPLE, INCLUDING ONE POLICEMAN, BEFORE HE HIMSELF WAS CUT DOWN BY POLICE BULLETS!

POLICE HAVE IDENTIFIED THE BODY AS ***JOSEF MACKY***, AN UNEMPLOYED FOLK SINGER, BUT HAVE SO FAR ESTABLISHED NO MOTIVE!

IT NEVER ENDS, DOES IT, SIR?

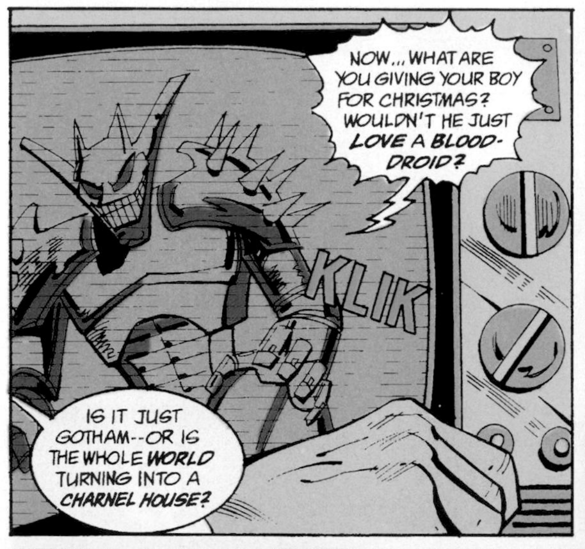
NOW... WHAT ARE YOU GIVING YOUR BOY FOR CHRISTMAS? WOULDN'T HE JUST LOVE A BLOOD-DROID?
KLIK
IS IT JUST GOTHAM--OR IS THE WHOLE WORLD TURNING INTO A CHARNEL HOUSE?

BEST NOT THINK ABOUT IT, ALFRED. YOU'LL ONLY GROW OLD FASTER!
STRANGE, THOUGH. ONE "CRIME OF WHIM" IS MORE THAN ENOUGH FOR ONE DAY. WHEN THEY START WEARING UNIFORMS, THERE HAS TO BE MORE TO IT!
I THINK I'LL--

SIR! YOU CAN'T! WE LEAVE IN FIVE MINUTES! MASTER TIM--
OF COURSE. THE HUMAN SKULLS WILL WAIT.
HAVE YOU SEEN HIM? HOW IS HE?

"BROKEN-HEARTED, SIR. ANGRY. CONFUSED. AFRAID."

YES. OF COURSE. I... REMEMBER ONLY TOO WELL.

MY MOTHER'S DEAD. DAD'LL SPEND THE REST OF HIS LIFE IN A CHAIR.
BOTH OF THEM--POISONED BY THE OBEAH MAN!

I HATE HIM! I HATE HIM!

I KNOW WHY THEY DO IT NOW. WHY THEY PUT ON THE SUITS, AND THE MASKS, AND GO OUT INTO THE NIGHT.
THEY'RE ANGRY. FULL OF RAGE. THEY WANT TO HIT BACK.

BAMP!
THEY WANT TO FILL THE HOLE THAT'S BURNING INSIDE THEM!
THERE'S MORE TO IT THAN THAT, SON.

MUCH MORE.
I KNOW.
IT'S JUST--I FEEL--LIKE GOING TO HAITI MYSELF AND STRANGLING THAT CREEP WITH MY BARE HANDS!
THE OBEAH MAN WILL SPEND THE REST OF HIS LIFE IN A PRISON HOSPITAL. HE'S HISTORY. FORGET HIM!
BUT DON'T FIGHT AGAINST YOUR ANGER. IT'S NATURAL. ACCEPT IT. LIVE WITH IT.

ONE DAY IT'LL BE YOUR FRIEND.

-- BIG COAT, AN' A HAT, AN A FACE LIKE A SKULL!
GCTV
GUY WAS CRAZY! SLICED UP FOZZY AN' TWO OF THE OTHERS BEFORE WE MANAGED TO PUSH HIM IN THE FIRE!
AN' GET THIS--HE'S A BUS DRIVER! WHAT THE HELL'S HE DOIN' WITH AN AX? WHY'S HE CHOPPIN' UP DOWN-AN'-OUTS?
MUST'VE HAPPENED JUST AFTER I LEFT THEM.
I'LL TELL YA WHY! WE'RE SCAPEGOATS FOR THIS WHOLE LOUSY CITY! FIGHT WITH THE BOSS? DON'T BOTTLE IT UP--GO DICE A SKEL!
KIDS ACTIN' UP? NO PROBLEM. GO SLICE A LOUSY HO--
ER, THANK YOU, MR.--ER...
HEY, DON'T BUTT IN ON ME, SISTER! I GOT RIGHTS, YA KNOW!
JUST LIKE THE MAN SAID! AND BEHIND HIM--THAT'S A CAR...
LET'S SEE IF I CAN BRING UP THE LICENSE PLATE.

THE CRUEL FATES, THE GREEKS CALLED THEM. THREE SISTERS WEAVING THE LOOM OF LIFE, SPINNING ITS GOLDEN THREADS INTO THE YEARS--
--CUTTING IT WHENEVER THE WHIM TOOK THEM.

JANET DRAKE
BELOVED WIFE OF JACK AND MOTHER OF TIM
STUPID!

BUT I GUESS WE ALL NEED SOMETHING TO HELP US MAKE SENSE OF IT ALL. WE NEED TO FIND MEANING IN THE PAIN... PATTERNS IN THE CHAOS.
JANET DRAKE

TIM NEEDS IT NOW, AS I ONCE NEEDED IT. AS BRUCE DID BEFORE ME.

SO WHY DO WE MAKE OUR FACES INTO MASKS? WHY DO WE HIDE THE PAIN WE ALL FEEL?

THANKS FOR COMING, DICK. I KNOW HOW BUSY--
IT WAS THE LEAST I COULD DO, TIM.
BELIEVE ME--I KNOW WHAT YOU'RE GOING THROUGH. IF YOU NEED ANY HELP, ANY TIME--

I APPRECIATE THAT. BUT...
I'LL COPE.

HE'S A BRAVE KID. HE'S IN CONTROL.
YOU KNOW WHAT COMES NEXT, DON'T YOU?
YES.

HE WANTS TO PUT ON THE SUIT.
AND...?

HE DOESN'T.

--WASTED YOUR TIME, MISS.
2BKU739
LT. KITCH
WE'VE CHECKED THE PLATE--REGISTERED TO A MR. RICO MARCUSE. HE WAS DRIVING BY THIS MORNING ON THE WAY TO HIS OFFICE. BUT HE DIDN'T SEE ANYTHING-- AND HE HAS NO CONNECTION WITH THE AX-KILLER.
OH.
IT'S JUST--I THOUGHT,,, MAYBE THEY WERE CONNECTED. YOU KNOW, LIKE THE CAR DROPPED THE KILLER OFF, OR SOMETHING...
YEAH. I KNOW. "BLOW-UP" WASN'T IT? SAW IT ON CABLE LAST WEEK.
AMPO
DO US A FAVOR, HUH? DON'T WATCH "NIGHTMARE ON ELM STREET" TONIGHT!
I FEEL RIDICULOUS. AND I WAS SO SURE I'D FOUND A CLUE!
GOTHAM PO
PH
STILL, WHAT'S TO SAY MR. RICO MARCUSE WASN'T LYING? I WOULD, IF I'D DROPPED OFF A KILLER!
PHONE

I WASTED A DAY ALREADY. I MIGHT AS WELL FOLLOW IT THROUGH!

BUT WHY NOT?

DANGER: FALLING ROCKS

I MEAN, YOU LET ME WORK ALL AFTERNOON WITH YOU TRYING TO FIND SOME *LINK* BETWEEN THESE KILLERS!

OKAY, SO IT HASN'T PANNED OUT YET. MAYBE THAT'S BECAUSE WE'VE MORE CHANCE OF FINDING THEM OUT ON THE *STREETS*.

SNK

SO WHY *CAN'T* I PUT ON THE SUIT AND COME WITH YOU?

YOU TELL *ME*.

DOES EVERYTHING HAVE TO BE A *TEST* WITH YOU?

ALL RIGHT, THEN--

WHEN YOU PUT ON THE SUIT YOU BECOME LARGER THAN LIFE. YOU BECOME A ***SYMBOL***.

AND THEN YOU DON'T HAVE A CHOICE. YOU ***HAVE*** TO LIVE UP TO WHAT YOU'VE MADE YOURSELF INTO.

THE MASK HIDES YOUR FEAR. NO ONE KNOWS WHAT YOU'RE THINKING.

AND IT'S DOUBLE-EDGED. IT FRIGHTENS YOUR ENEMIES AND FEEDS YOUR STRENGTH.

BUT ***NO*** SUIT-- ***NO*** MASK--CAN ***EVER*** HIDE ***YOU*** FROM ***YOURSELF!***

I DON'T UNDERSTAND...

PERHAPS WHEN YOU DO, THAT'LL BE THE TIME.

NO! IF I LISTEN TO YOU, I'LL NEVER DO IT!
I'M READY NOW! I CAN FEEL IT-- HERE! I'M NOT A KID ANY MORE. I'M READY!

BATMAN, PLEASE--!
NO.

THAT'S MY FINAL WORD. DISOBEY ME--

--AND YOU CAN FORGET ABOUT EVER BEING ROBIN!
VRRRMMMMM

HE'S WRONG. I AM READY. I KNOW IT.
BUT ARGUING WON'T CHANGE HIS MIND. HE'S THE BOSS.

I GUESS I'LL
JUST HAVE TO
SHOW HIM!

THIS IS IT, ALL RIGHT.
LUCKY I CHECKED HIS
BUSINESS FIRST.

THAT'S
PROBABLY
HIM THERE.
SO WHAT DO YOU DO NOW,
VICKI? GO IN AND ASK HIM?
FOLLOW THE CAR WHEN HE
COMES OUT?

HMM. I GUESS I SHOULD HAVE
THOUGHT ABOUT THIS. WHY WOULD
A RICH BUSINESSMAN BE FERRYING
ROUND A KILLER ANY--

--WAY?
OH--!

NEXT ISSUE:
"THE HEART OF A HERO"

BATMAN

GRANT
BREYFOGLE
MITCHELL

Cover art by Norm Breyfogle

IDENTITY CRISIS PART TWO:
WITHOUT FEAR OF CONSEQUENCE...
BATMAN
MERRY CHRISTMAS, SUCKERS! HO HO HO!
EY'S
GRACEY
"The donning of a mask is believed to change a man's identity and faculties, for the assumed appearance is held to affect the wearer's inner nature and to assimilate it to that of the being represented by the mask." --ENCYCLOPEDIA OF MAGIC AND SUPERSTITION
ALAN GRANT WRITER
NORM BREYFOGLE PENCILLER
STEVE MITCHELL INKER
ADRIENNE ROY COLORIST
TODD KLEIN LETTERER
KELLEY PUCKETT asst. EDITOR
DENNIS O'NEIL EDITOR
BOB KANE CREATOR

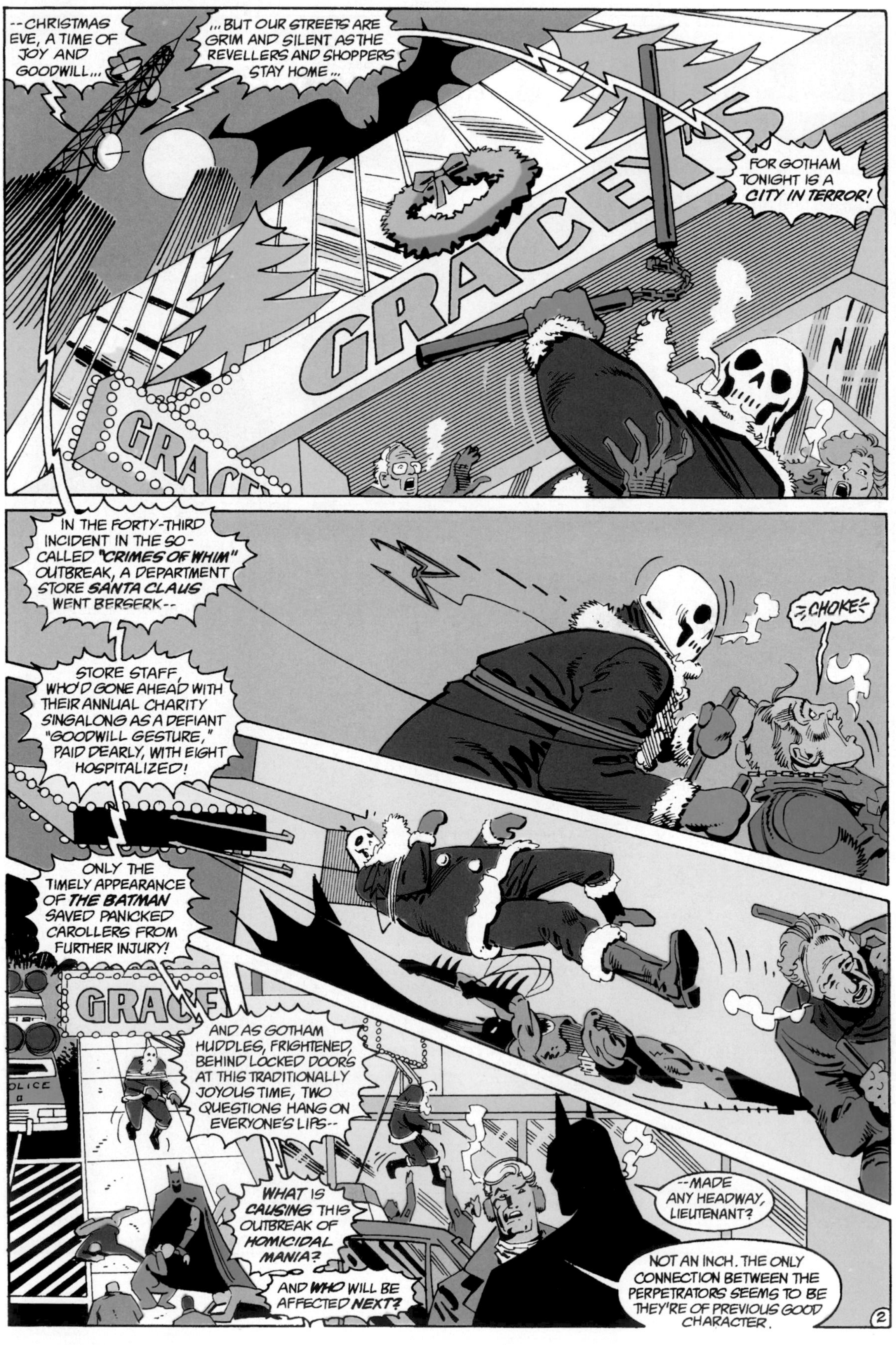

--CHRISTMAS EVE, A TIME OF JOY AND GOODWILL...
...BUT OUR STREETS ARE GRIM AND SILENT AS THE REVELLERS AND SHOPPERS STAY HOME...
FOR GOTHAM TONIGHT IS A CITY IN TERROR!
GRACEY'S
GRACE
IN THE FORTY-THIRD INCIDENT IN THE SO-CALLED "CRIMES OF WHIM" OUTBREAK, A DEPARTMENT STORE SANTA CLAUS WENT BERSERK--
CHOKE
STORE STAFF, WHO'D GONE AHEAD WITH THEIR ANNUAL CHARITY SINGALONG AS A DEFIANT "GOODWILL GESTURE," PAID DEARLY, WITH EIGHT HOSPITALIZED!
ONLY THE TIMELY APPEARANCE OF THE BATMAN SAVED PANICKED CAROLLERS FROM FURTHER INJURY!
GRACE
AND AS GOTHAM HUDDLES, FRIGHTENED, BEHIND LOCKED DOORS AT THIS TRADITIONALLY JOYOUS TIME, TWO QUESTIONS HANG ON EVERYONE'S LIPS--
OLICE
WHAT IS CAUSING THIS OUTBREAK OF HOMICIDAL MANIA?
AND WHO WILL BE AFFECTED NEXT?
--MADE ANY HEADWAY, LIEUTENANT?
NOT AN INCH. THE ONLY CONNECTION BETWEEN THE PERPETRATORS SEEMS TO BE THEY'RE OF PREVIOUS GOOD CHARACTER.

YOU'VE TAKEN BLOOD SAMPLES? TESTED FOR TOXINS?
FORENSICS IS ON 24-HOUR OVERTIME. ALL THEIR TESTS SAY ZILCH! NO GO ON THE HYPNOSIS FRONT, EITHER.

IN FACT, CLOSEST WE'VE COME TO A LEAD WAS A CLAIM FROM A MISS VALE --
VICKI VALE? THE PHOTOGRAPHER?
YEAH. SHE'D BEEN WATCHING ONE OF THOSE OLD '60'S MOVIES, FIGURED SHE'D FOUND A CLUE IN A PICTURE SHE TOOK.

'COURSE IT WAS ALL A FANTASY. GUY SHE SUSPECTED CHECKED OUT CLEAN.
MIND TELLING ME WHO...?
A MR. MARCUSE -- RUNS A FUR BUSINESS OVER ON DEERE STREET. UPRIGHT, RESPECTABLE CITIZEN.

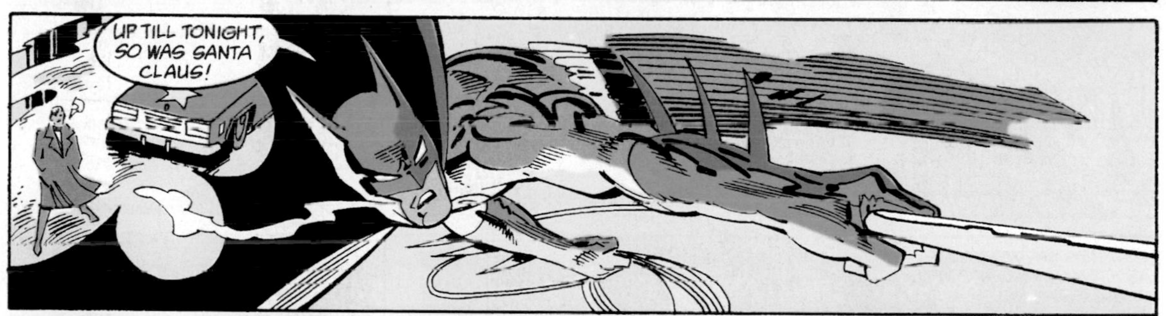
UP TILL TONIGHT, SO WAS SANTA CLAUS!

GOTHAM'S A GHOST TOWN. THE BRIGHT LIGHTS PLAY TO EMPTY STREETS. SILENCE HANGS LIKE A SHROUD.

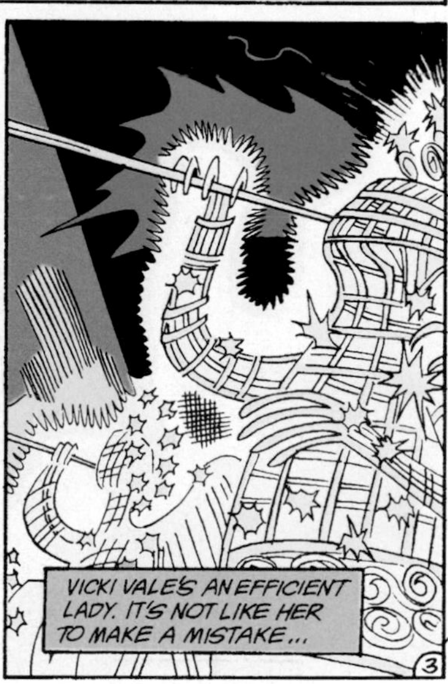
VICKI VALE'S AN EFFICIENT LADY. IT'S NOT LIKE HER TO MAKE A MISTAKE...

THOUGH IT IS JUST LIKE HER TO STICK HER NOSE IN WHERE IT ISN'T NEEDED!
KRAK!

--BOWDLER, VINCENT S., 334 EAST RIVER APARTMENTS.
GOT IT, MR. MARCUSE!

THAT'S THE LAST THREE. BETTER GET GOING--I SAID THEY'D ALL BE DONE BY MIDNIGHT!
LOOKS LIKE YAZZ HAS CAUGHT A SNOOPER, MR. M!

IT SEEMS MY SUSPICIONS ABOUT MARCUSE ARE WELL-FOUNDED--THOUGH A FAT LOT OF GOOD THAT'LL DO ME AGAINST THIS PSYCHO!

SMASH
OHH--!

D-DON'T COME ANY CLOSER! I'M WARNING YOU--!
ALL RIGHT, YAZZ. I'LL TAKE CARE OF THIS.
4

WHAT YOU DOING, WEARING THAT THING ANYHOW?
JUST HAVIN' A LITTLE FUN, MR. MARCUSE! I CAUGHT HER CHECKIN' OUT YOUR CAR.

ALL RIGHT. GET THAT STUFF DELIVERED.
AND NO FOUL-UPS!

HEY, BOSS--THIS IS A PRESS CARD! SHE'S A JOURNALIST!
I REMEMBER YOU NOW. THE BUMS THIS MORNING...!
I GUESS I SHOULDN'T HAVE GONE THERE. THOUGH I HAD TO BE SURE IT WORKED, YOU UNDERSTAND.

I DON'T KNOW WHAT YOU'RE TALKING ABOUT, MISTER!
I WAS OUT FOR A WALK WHEN THE GOON IN THE DEATH-MASK ATTACKED ME. YOU BETTER HAVE A GOOD LAWYER, PAL, BECAUSE I'M GOING TO SUE--

PERHAPS YOU'RE TELLING THE TRUTH. PERHAPS NOT. WHICHEVER, IT'S TOO LATE NOW.
PUT HER IN THE CAR!
YOU CAN'T DO THIS! WHERE ARE YOU TAKING ME?
TO SEE A MAN, MISS VALE...

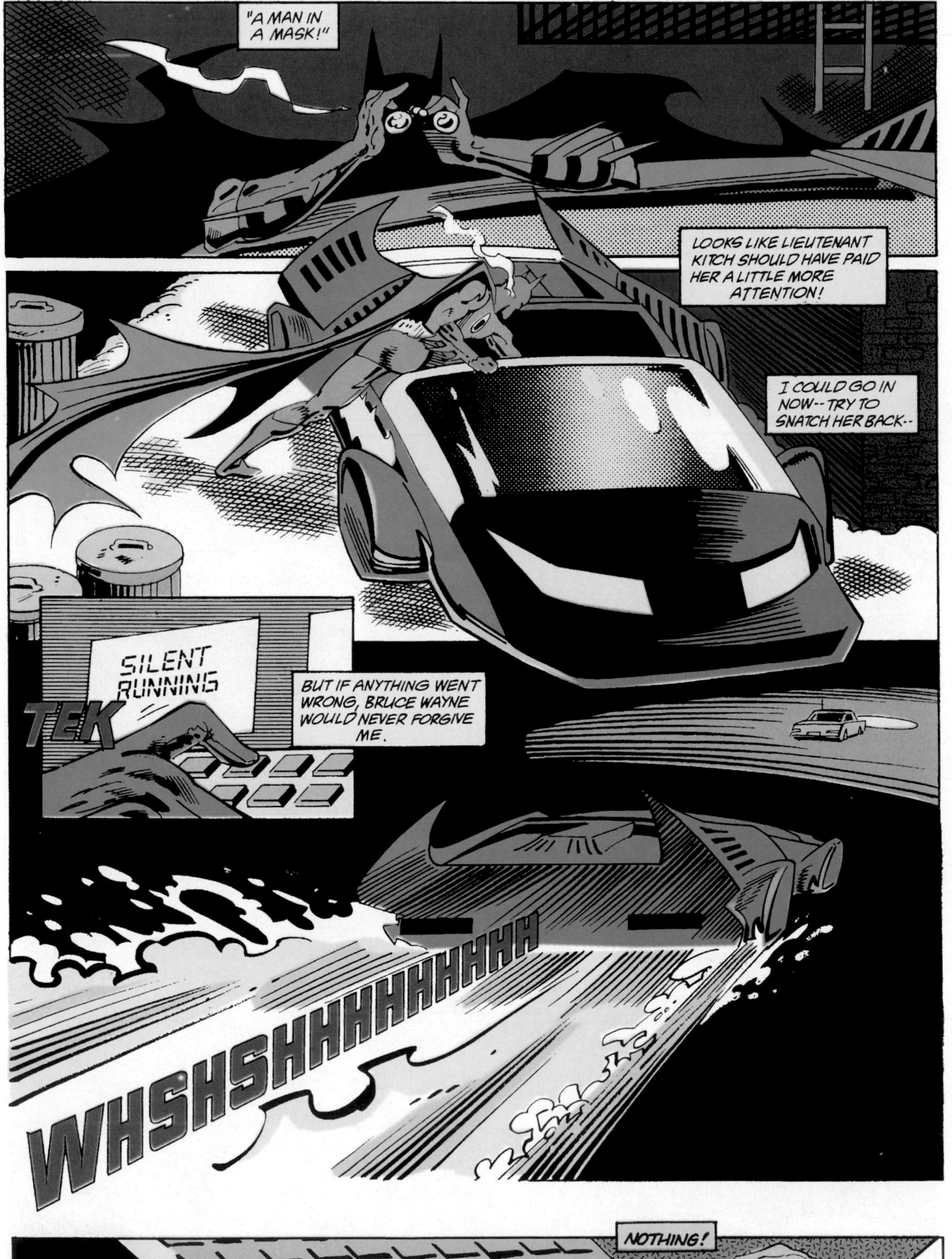
"A MAN IN A MASK!"
LOOKS LIKE LIEUTENANT KITCH SHOULD HAVE PAID HER A LITTLE MORE ATTENTION!
I COULD GO IN NOW-- TRY TO SNATCH HER BACK--
SILENT RUNNING
TEK
BUT IF ANYTHING WENT WRONG, BRUCE WAYNE WOULD NEVER FORGIVE ME.
WHSHSHHHHHHHHHH
NOTHING!

I've cross-referenced every scrap of data on the people who commited those crimes--and there's absolutely no common link!
It's as if they all had homicidal breakdowns --at random, but at the same time... and that just doesn't make sense.
TAK AKAK AKAK AKAKAKAK
The crimes--random killing by ordinary people--and the death-mask imagery don't fit with any of Batman's regular foes--
--any more than they do with the dozens of minor criminals he's faced.

I thought when Batman forbade me to wear the suit, I could prove I'd **earned** the right by solving this crime for him. But it's just not working out.

At this rate, there's **never** going to be another Robin!

AHEM!
OH. HI, ALFRED!

BROODING ON WHAT CANNOT BE IS NO WAY FOR A BOY TO SPEND CHRISTMAS EVE, MASTER TIM!
I WONDERED IF PERHAPS YOU'D LIKE TO HELP ME WRAP SOME PRESENTS...?

CHRISTMAS...! I'D COMPLETELY FORGOTTEN, WHAT WITH MY MOTHER'S-- WITH THE FUNERAL, AND THE MURDERS IN THE CITY!
I COULD SURE USE A BREAK...

...BUT I CAN'T AFFORD ONE. GUESS I'LL HAVE TO SIT CHRISTMAS OUT THIS YEAR.
CONGRATULATIONS, SIR. I'M SURE IT'LL BE THE FIRST OF MANY!
8

THERE'S AN ANSWER TO THIS MYSTERY SOMEWHERE--
--AND IF BATMAN'S EVER GOING TO ACCEPT ME, I HAVE TO FIND IT!
The suit! If only I could...
The suit is magic. It gives you power. It hides your weakness. It makes you give it everything you've got.
It makes you a hero.
If only I could!
Think, Tim! What makes a grandmother shoot four men--on a whim? What makes a man turn on people he's worked with for years?
THINK!

SAVOR IT. A WHOLE CITY-- EIGHT MILLION PEOPLE! EIGHT MILLION!
IN TERROR!

VVRRRRMMMM

TERROR. EXTREME FEAR. A HORRIBLY PAINFUL EMOTION CAUSED BY IMPENDING DANGER OR EVIL.

WSHSHHHHHHHHHHHHHH

EIGHT MILLION...

OH, SAVOR IT!
GOTHAM CHEMICAL
WEIRDEST JOB I EVER HAD--

GUARDIN' AN ABANDONED FACTORY WHILE A GUY JUST SITS INSIDE.
WHO CARES? HIS MONEY'S GOOD, AIN'T IT?
LIGHTS!

'S OKAY! IT'S MARCUSE!

WHAT'S THE GAME, MARCUSE? BOSS NEVER SAID HE WAS EXPECTIN' YOU BACK.
SOMETHIN' TURNED UP-- WHAT ABOUT THE DAME?

WAIT. I'LL SEE WHAT HE SAYS.
COMPANY! I HAD BETTER DRESS.

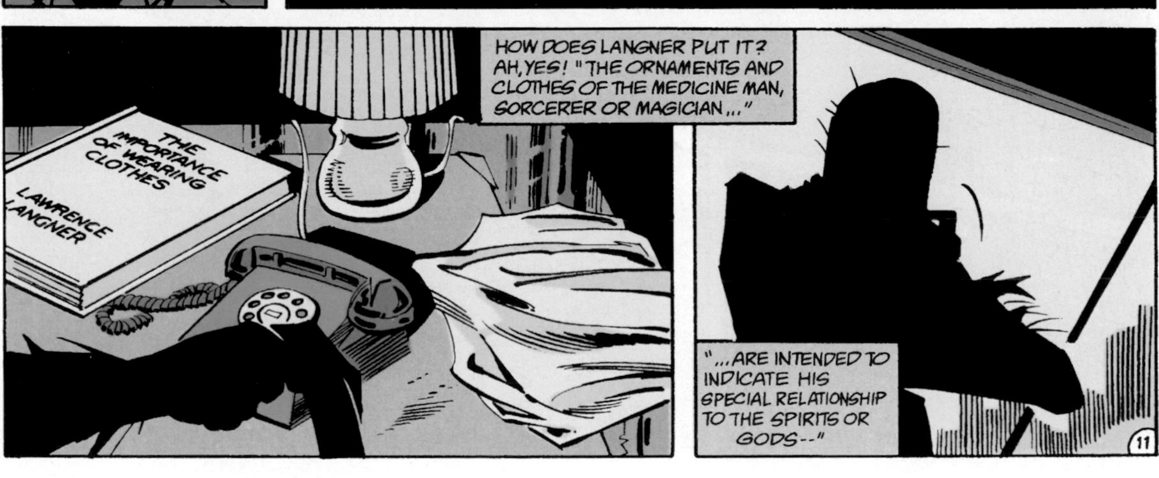
HOW DOES LANGNER PUT IT? AH, YES! "THE ORNAMENTS AND CLOTHES OF THE MEDICINE MAN, SORCERER OR MAGICIAN..."
THE IMPORTANCE OF WEARING CLOTHES
LAWRENCE LANGNER
"...ARE INTENDED TO INDICATE HIS SPECIAL RELATIONSHIP TO THE SPIRITS OR GODS--"

"AND HIS CONTROL OR POWER OVER THEM."
HOOOAAAAAAARRR

YOU RATS! I'LL SEE YOU'RE ALL JAILED FOR THIS!
QUIT STRUGGLIN', SWEETHEART--

MMMFFFFNGH!
BOOT

OUTA THE WAY, JAKE!
IF I CAN FIND A WINDOW TO THE OUTSIDE--

STAIRS
BLAST! WHICH ONE?
TAKE A CHANCE, VICKI--
OHH--!
Y-Y-YOU...!

What's a whim, anyway? An unaccountable change of mind. Caprice. Doing something without forethought... without fear of consequences.

1947

What whim makes nearly fifty people into **murderers**? What--or **who**...?

Blast it! My head's starting to **swim.** I'm about ready to give up. I almost wish I'd never **heard** of Batman and Robin!

HEROES NEVER GIVE UP, TIM.

YOU KNOW THAT.

DICK--! JASON TODD!

THINK, TIM. CONCENTRATE!
YOU CAN DO IT.

YOU CAN DO IT!
YOU CAN DO IT!

WHAT--?
ROBIN...?

I must have been daydreaming.
They're right, though. There's a solution to everything. I can find it!
IN MEMORY OF JASON TODD ROBIN A GOOD SOLDIER

So here I go again...
Whim. Caprice. Doing something without forethought...

Without fear of consequence...
Of course! That's it--
FEAR!

BRNNNG

BRNNGG

--ANOTHER TWO, COMMISSIONER!
GOTHAM POL
GOTHAM POLICE DEPT.

A VINCE BOWDLER SET FIRE TO HIS PARENTS' HOUSE OVER ON EAST RIVER. IT'S SPREAD TO THE WHOLE BLOCK. AND A T.V. REPAIRMAN'S HOLDING SIX HOSTAGES ON PARKSIDE.
IT JUST DOESN'T MAKE ANY SENSE, KITCH!

NO THREATS--NO RANSOM DEMANDS. IT'S ALMOST AS IF IT'S... A NATURAL OCCURRENCE!
EXCUSE ME. YES, GORDON SPEAKING--

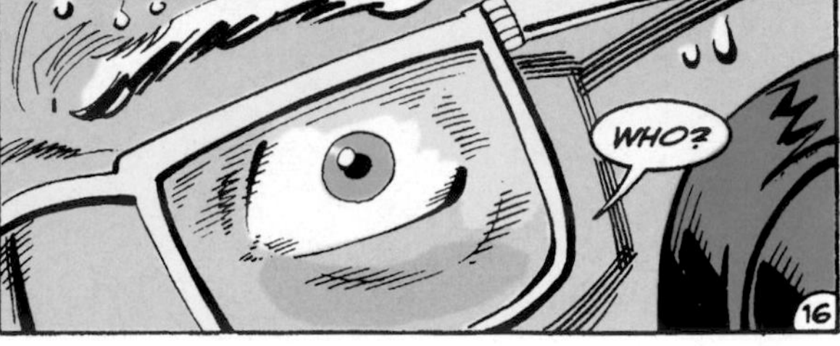
WHO?

I THINK YOU HEARD, SIR.
I BELIEVE I KNOW WHO'S BEHIND THE DEATH-MASK CRIMES-- BUT BATMAN DOESN'T. THERE'S NO RESPONSE FROM THE BATMOBILE.

I ... WANT YOU TO PUT UP THE SIGNAL.
WHY? EXACTLY WHO DO YOU THINK IS RESPONSIBLE?
OH.

BUT WHY? WHY ARE YOU DOING THIS?
GOTHAM CHEMICAL

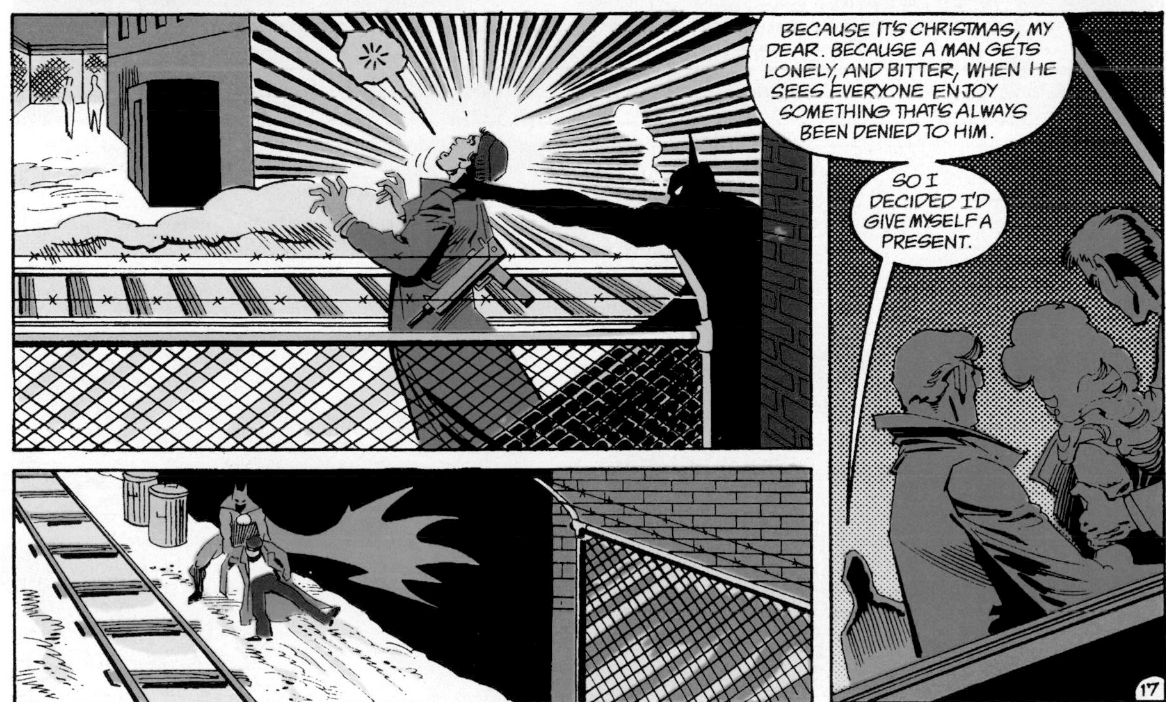
BECAUSE IT'S CHRISTMAS, MY DEAR. BECAUSE A MAN GETS LONELY, AND BITTER, WHEN HE SEES EVERYONE ENJOY SOMETHING THAT'S ALWAYS BEEN DENIED TO HIM.
SO I DECIDED I'D GIVE MYSELF A PRESENT.

THE SIGNAL! EXCELLENT!

COULDN'T NEED ME AT A WORSE TIME.

HAVE THEY REALIZED IT'S *ME*, DO YOU THINK? OR JUST ANOTHER WHIM-KILLING?

NO MATTER. IT'LL SOON BE CHRISTMAS.

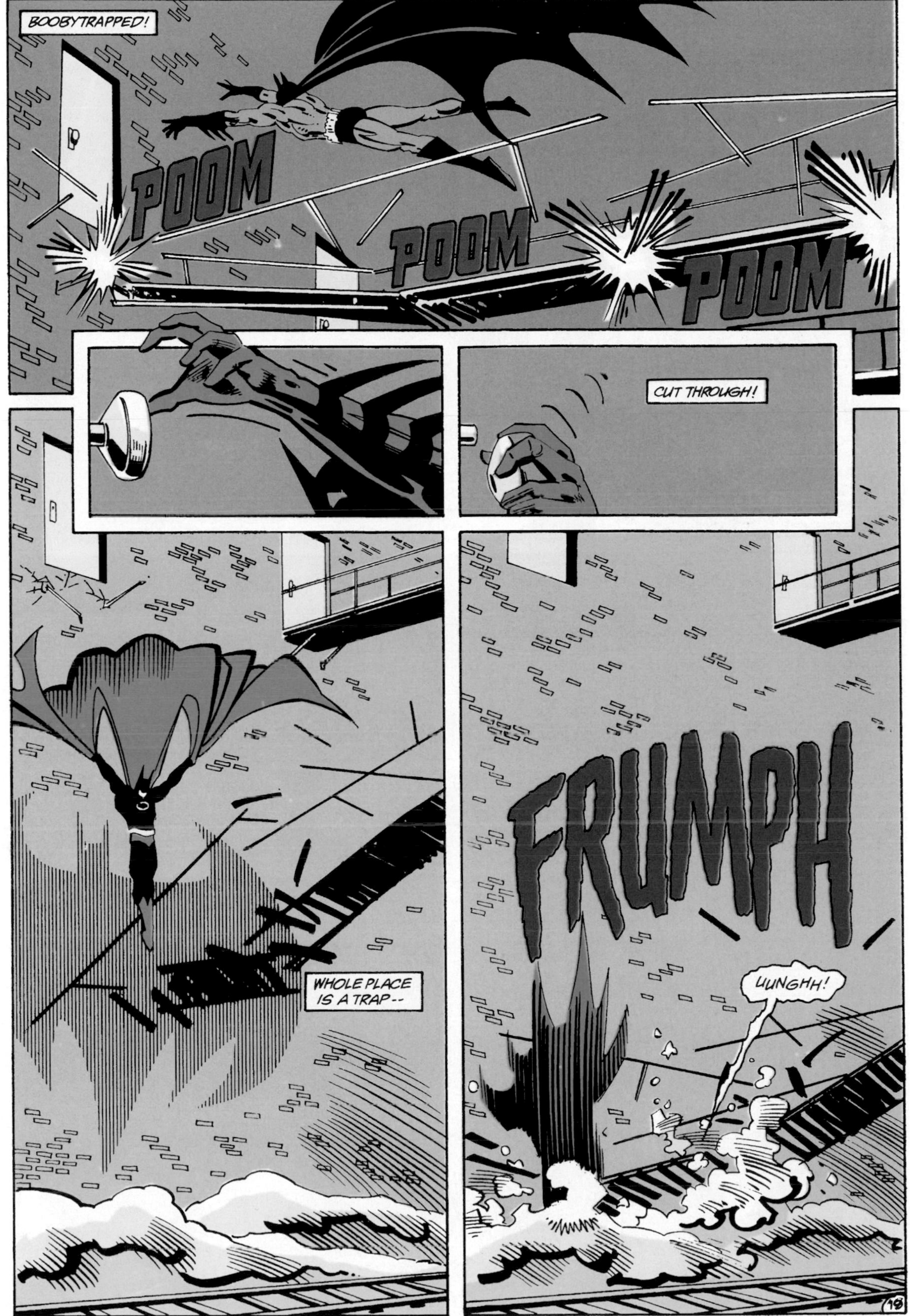
BOOBYTRAPPED!
POOM
POOM
POOM
CUT THROUGH!
WHOLE PLACE IS A TRAP--
FRUMPH
UUNGHH!

--LAST TIME THEY MET HE WAS USING AN OLD FACTORY OUT IN THE INDUSTRIAL AREA. COULD YOU SEND UNITS OUT THERE RIGHT AWAY?
LISTEN, ROBIN--IF THAT'S WHO YOU REALLY *ARE!* I'VE A MAJOR FIRE AND A HOSTAGE SITUATION IN PROGRESS-- AND GOD KNOWS WHAT *ELSE* BY NOW!
I CAN'T PULL MEN AWAY ON SOME THOUSAND-TO-ONE SHOT. I'LL SEND A CAR AS SOON AS I CAN.
MEANTIME, DON'T WORRY. BATMAN CAN LOOK AFTER HIMSELF.
YES, SIR. I UNDERSTAND.

I guess I wait.
Batman will be all right.
He's always all right.
SLAM
MASTER TIM!
SORRY, ALFRED!
WHERE ON EARTH ARE YOU GOING--?
TAXI
TO SAY GOODBYE TO MY CHANCES OF EVER BEING HIS PARTNER!
I'VE BEEN WAITING, BATMAN. I KNEW YOU'D FIND ME. YOU ALWAYS DO.

HOOOHOHOOOOOAAAAHAAA
AND NOW MY CHRISTMAS IS COMPLETE!
HAAAARRR
NEXT ISSUE: MASTER OF FEAR!

DC
BATMAN
457
US $1.00
CAN $1.25
DEC 90
GRANT • BREYFOGLE • MITCHELL

Cover art by Norm Breyfogle

MASTER of FEAR
HOAAAAAHAAAARRRRRR
"The wearer of the mask partakes of the power of the divinity or spirit which the mask symbolizes..."
--ENCYCLOPEDIA OF MAGIC AND SUPERSTITION
ALAN GRANT WRITER
NORM BREYFOGLE PENCILLER
STEVE MITCHELL INKER
ADRIENNE ROY COLORIST
TODD KLEIN LETTERER
KELLEY PUCKETT ASST. ED.
DENNIS O'NEIL EDITOR
BOB KANE CREATOR
SPECIAL THANKS TO KEVIN BREYFOGLE

...A CITY IN TERROR IS A GREAT THING--BUT IT WAS ONLY A MEANS TO AN END.
CHEST'S ON FIRE. HURTS TO BREATHE. AT LEAST ONE RIB CRACKED FOR SURE.
DEEP CUT, LEFT ARM. SHOULDER WAS WRENCHED IN THE FALL. I'LL BE A MASS OF BRUISES TOMORROW...
A TRAP FOR YOU, BATMAN! THE ULTIMATE CHRISTMAS PRESENT TO MYSELF!
IF THERE IS A TOMORROW!
THIS IS INSANE, SCARECROW! WHAT DO YOU HOPE TO GAIN...?
A WARM GLOW. THE PLEASURE OF SLOWLY...
...UNWRAPPING YOU!
SO--YOU WANT ME, YOU'VE GOT ME! WHY NOT LET THE GIRL GO?
NEVER CHANGE, DO YOU? SAME TIRED OLD CONCERN FOR THE WEAK AND INNOCENT.
BUT MISS VICKI VALE ISN'T QUITE THE INNO-CENT. SHE'S A JOURNALIST.
SHE WAS INVESTIGATING MY HIRELINGS. RATHER STUPIDLY, THEY BROUGHT HER HERE!
2

I TOLD YOU, SCARECROW-- WE THOUGHT YOU'D WANT TO FIND OUT WHAT SHE KNOWS!
THINKING IS FOR PEOPLE WITH BRAINS, MARCUSE. REMEMBER THAT, IF WE HAVE DEALINGS AGAIN.

HOWEVER, YOU DID YOUR JOB WELL. HERE IS THE BONUS I PROMISED.
NOW TAKE YOUR MEN AND GO MAKE MERRY!
YES, SIR!

CREEP THAT TIED ME KNEW HIS STUFF. TWO CORDS. THIS ISN'T GOING TO BE EASY.
AS FOR YOU, MISS VALE--I'M SURE I'LL THINK OF SOMETHING-- INTERESTING!

SCARECROW-- JUST WHAT IS THIS ALL ABOUT?
A WHIM, BATMAN. A SIMPLE, HONEST-TO-GOODNESS WHIM!

YOU SEE, WHEN I WAS A BOY, I LIKED TO FRIGHTEN BIRDS...
IT WAS A WHIM, THAT FIRST TIME--A SPUR-OF-THE-MOMENT CAPRICE.
"THE SHEER, UNADULTERATED PLEASURE I FELT IN THEIR TERROR WAS TO SHAPE MY WHOLE LIFE!
3

"YEARS LATER IT WAS *WHIM* CAUSED ME TO PULL THAT *GUN* IN MY PSYCHOLOGY CLASS.

BLAM!

CHSH

"AND THE *FEAR* IT PRODUCED WAS *SWEETER* THAN ANYTHING I HAD KNOWN!

"AND WHEN FINALLY--PROVOKED BY THOSE BOORS WHO THOUGHT THEMSELVES MY *BETTER*--I DECIDED ON A LIFE OF *CRIME*--"

IT WAS *WHIM* MADE ME CHOOSE THE NAME AND IMAGE THEY HAD SO CALLOUSLY CAST ON ME--

THE SCARECROW-- A BEING WHOSE SOLE RAISON D'ETRE IS TO *FRIGHTEN*!

I'VE LEARNED TO *FOLLOW* MY WHIMS, BATMAN!

SO FAR, IN FACT, THAT I'VE CREATED A *HYPNOTIC* DRUG.

THAT'S WHAT CAUSED NORMAL PEOPLE TO KILL. HARD TO BELIEVE.

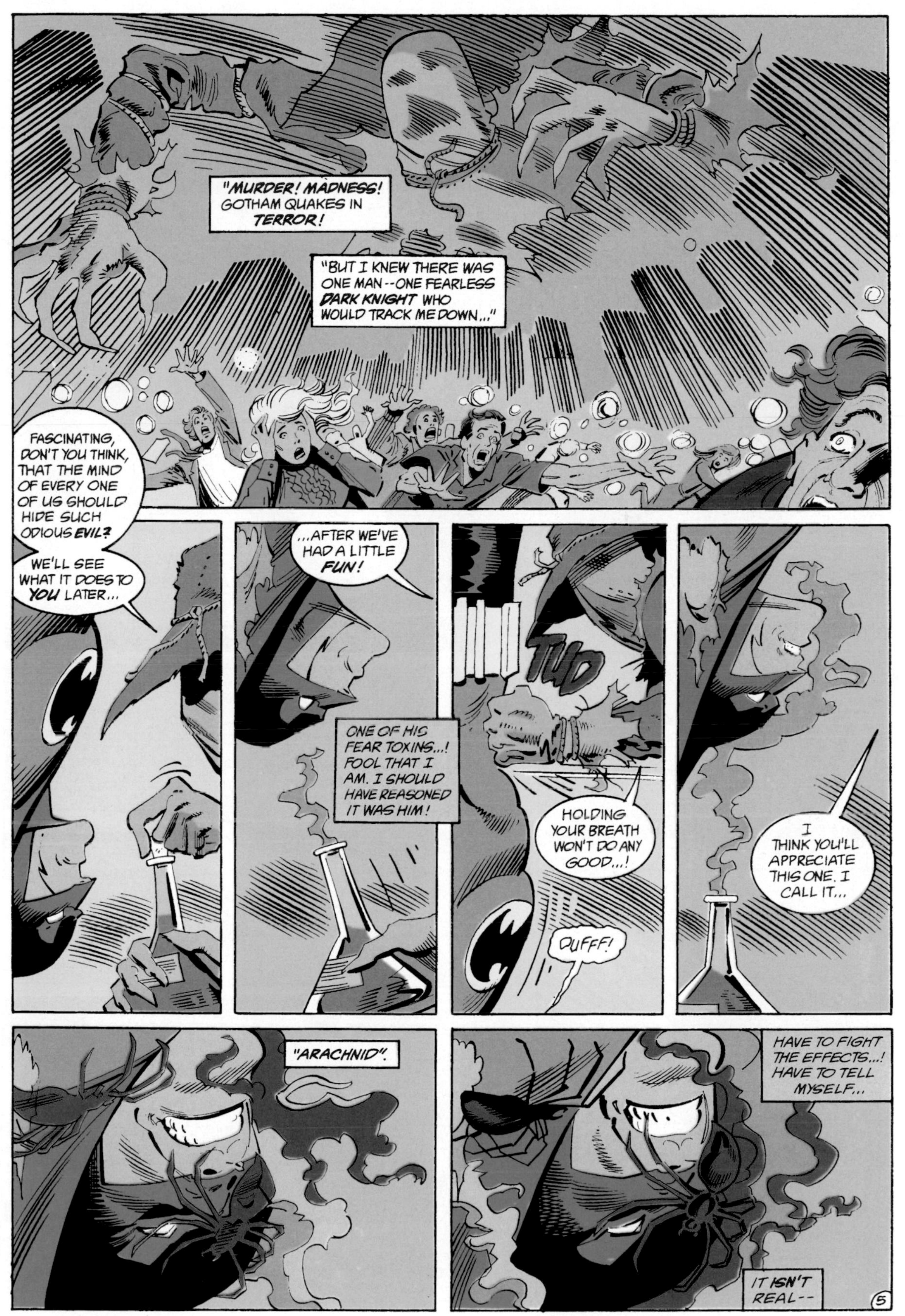
"MURDER! MADNESS! GOTHAM QUAKES IN TERROR!
"BUT I KNEW THERE WAS ONE MAN--ONE FEARLESS DARK KNIGHT WHO WOULD TRACK ME DOWN..."
FASCINATING, DON'T YOU THINK, THAT THE MIND OF EVERY ONE OF US SHOULD HIDE SUCH ODIOUS EVIL?
WE'LL SEE WHAT IT DOES TO YOU LATER...
...AFTER WE'VE HAD A LITTLE FUN!
ONE OF HIS FEAR TOXINS...! FOOL THAT I AM. I SHOULD HAVE REASONED IT WAS HIM!
TUD
HOLDING YOUR BREATH WON'T DO ANY GOOD...!
OUFFF!
I THINK YOU'LL APPRECIATE THIS ONE. I CALL IT...
"ARACHNID".
HAVE TO FIGHT THE EFFECTS...! HAVE TO TELL MYSELF...
IT ISN'T REAL--

--IT ISN'T REAL!

--FIRST FARE I HAD ALL NIGHT, KID. CITY'S SO SCARED, THEY'RE ALL STAYIN' HOME TO WATCH CHRISTMAS ON T.V.!
LAMPSON CONSTRUCTION

ANOTHER CAR! WHAT'S GOIN' ON--SOME KIND OF WAREHOUSE PARTY?
uh... SOMETHING LIKE THAT.

GOTHAM CHEMICAL
Looks like I was right! Why would anyone else be out here at this time of night?
TAXI

A CAB? WHERE THE HECK'S THAT GOIN'?
HOW DO I KNOW? MAYBE THE SCARECROW SENT OUT FOR PIZZA!

TEN THOU BONUS THAT MANIAC PROMISED US. BETTER THAN SELLIN' FURS ANY--
HUH?
PHHT
DIE! DIE!
IT'S A DOUBLE-CROSS! THAT'S THE SCARECROW'S GAS--!
SKREEEEEEEE
BOSS! LET HIM GO! WE'RE GONNA--
SKRAANG
FRUMPH
DANGER TOXIC WASTE
AAUGHH!
KRANG
SPLASH
IT'S DESERTED! YOU SURE ABOUT THIS, KID?
YES. I'M... MEETING SOME PEOPLE.
No time to waste. If I am right-- if this is a Scarecrow scam--Batman's in deadly danger!
7

He'd have used the Batmobile. Where would he park it?
Somewhere hidden-- but close enough for a quick getaway--

I'd rather have been **wrong**!

So... this is it. He gave me a direct order to stay put.
Just **being** here is the end of my quest to become his partner!

SOME WAY T' SPEND XMAS, HAMMY!
AH, THE MONEY'S GOOD.
CALOR GAS EXPLOSIVE
But what else **can** I do?
'SIDES, IT'S NICE TO SEE THE BOSS *ENJOYIN'* HIMSELF!
CALOR GAS EXPLOSIVE
Too big and hard for me to tackle. Armed, anyway.
I'll just have to improvise--

KLANGG
WHAT WAS THAT?
JUST A CAT OR SOMETHIN'!

OH YEAH? WEARIN' BOOTS, MAYBE?
C'MON!
KLANGG

AWRIGHT! WHOEVER'S IN THERE, I'M GONNA COUNT T' THREE...
ONE!

TWO!

SLAM!
HEY--!

'S WEDGED! I CAN'T BUDGE IT!
THEN WE'LL SHOOT IT OPEN!

NO NAKED FLAME
LIQUID GAS
NO NAKED FLAME
LIQUID GAS
NO NAKED FLAME
UH, I DON'T THINK SO, HAMMY...!

COMING OUT OF IT? FINE. LET'S JUST SEE WHAT ELSE...
YOU MONSTER!

PSSSST!

HAMMY? LEON...?

YOU THERE, GU--

--UUHH!

Tripwire worked--but he's only dazed!

KLUNK!

I hoped I wouldn't have to do this--!

ANYTHING IN YOUR CHILDHOOD YOU'D RATHER NOT REMEMBER...?
BLOOD'S POUNDING IN MY HEAD. CAN'T THINK STRAIGHT. DON'T SEE ANY WAY...
At least he's still alive!
Only one way in...
But not like this. If I'm recognized, it could lead straight back to Bruce Wayne!
FIGHT IT ALL YOU LIKE, BATMAN-- IT WON'T MATTER IN THE END!
BY MORNING, I'LL HAVE PEELED AWAY EVERYTHING YOU ARE...
AND THEN I'LL FIND OUT WHAT DEMONIC THOUGHTS YOU'VE SPENT YOUR MISERABLE LIFE REPRESSING!
NOT THIS!
CRIME ALLEY
DEAR LORD, NOT THIS!

JONATHAN CRANE-- SCARECROW!
STEP AWAY FROM HIM-- NOW!
AND WHO ARE YOU, MY DWARFISH FRIEND?
NONE OF YOUR CONCERN! CUT HIM DOWN!
AAAH!
WHAT--?
Careless! I should have made sure--
SLAM!
IMPRESSIVE WORK. HERE-- HAVE YOUR REWARD!
AND YOU, MISS VALE--!
SPSH

It's some sort of fear gas! "Trauma" he called it! Can feel it already--
The Obeah Man! Mom--Dad... he's killing them!
Dejection--failure--fear... like weights in my mind, dragging me down--
I have to fight...!
I have to--
No! NO!
...MY PUPPY! YOU RAN OVER MY PUPPY...!
AHH... FEAR! ITS ESSENCE IS ALMOST PALPABLE...!
MERRY CHRISTMAS, JONATHAN!
HOAAARRRRRRRR
I'M NOT AFRAID! I'M NOT! I'M NOT! I'M NOT!
13

Fear-- dirty shadows squeezing my mind... I can't stop the Obeah Man! I'm a failure!
LOOK AT HIM! PARALYZED WITH FEAR!
DON'T FIGHT IT, TIM! LIVE WITH IT! CONFRONT IT!
IT'S NOTHING TO BE ASHAMED OF. BUT JUST BECAUSE YOU'RE AFRAID--
--DOESN'T MEAN YOU CAN'T ACT!
YOU DON'T NEED THE SUIT! YOU DON'T NEED THE MASK!
IT'S IN YOU! YOU MAKE YOURSELF A HERO!
SO... WHAT NOW, BATMAN? "BURIED ALIVE"? "EATEN BY ROACHES... FROM THE INSIDE"?
I can do it! I know I can!
I DON'T CARE IF I AM AFRAID--

WUMMP!
I CAN STILL ACT!
SMASHH!
CHSH
MY TOXINS--!
AAAH!
Got to get clear--
CRASHHH!
N-NO--KEEP AWAY!

KEEP AWAY! LEAVE ME ALONE!
AIEEEEEEEEEEEEEEEEEEEE
BATMAN...?
BATMAN...!
ROBIN...?

GOTHAM CHEMICAL
--MAYBE THE CABBY WAS DRUNK!
I MEAN, WHAT WOULD A KID BE DOIN' OUT HERE AT MIDNIGHT ON CHRISTMAS..?
THAT'S WHAT WE'RE GONNA FIND OUT!
SHOOT! SOMETHIN'S GOIN' ON!
MORE LIKE A WAR THAN A WAREHOUSE PARTY, THOUGH!
GCPD
WELL, I'LL BE--!
GCPD

DON'T HURT ME! PLEASE--!
--ALL THE BLOOD EVERYWHERE--
IT'S OKAY, VICKI. YOU'LL BE ALL RIGHT.

No, not Robin. Not now. Not ever.

But at least he's alive!

GET MISS VALE TO THE HOSPITAL. LOCK HIM UP.
STAIRS
THEY'LL BOTH COME BACK TO NORMAL AS SOON AS THE DRUG WEARS OFF.

YOU DON'T LOOK IN GREAT SHAPE YOURSELF, BATMAN! YOU WANT TO COME--?
POLICE
I'VE OTHER BUSINESS.

THEY'VE GONE.

ARE YOU OKAY?
STILL A BIT... WOOZY. BUT-- IT'S WEARING OFF.

WHAT DID I TELL YOU?
TO STAY HOME.
BUT--I FIGURED IT WAS THE SCARECROW. I KNEW YOU WERE WALKING INTO A TRAP!

I'M SORRY. I KNOW IT MEANS I'LL NEVER BE YOUR PARTNER. I'LL NEVER WEAR THE SUIT.
WHY DIDN'T YOU WEAR IT TONIGHT?
I THOUGHT-- IF I FAILED, I'D DISGRACE IT.

I COULDN'T LIVE WITH THAT.

YOU'VE LEARNED SOME-THING VALUABLE, SON.
SURE, WE MAKE UP THE RULES, AND THEN WE HAVE TO STICK TO THEM. BUT SOMETIMES A HUNCH-- A FEELING IN YOUR GUT-- MAKES YOU THINK AGAIN.

SOMETIMES--NOT VERY OFTEN, AND ONLY WHEN IT'S JUSTIFIED-- A HERO GETS TO BREAK THE RULES.
IF YOU HADN'T, VICKI VALE AND I WOULD BOTH BE DEAD.
13

THANKS...
...ROBIN.

ARE YOU AFRAID OF IT?
NO. IT ISN'T FEAR. IT'S MORE... THE SUIT CARRIES SO MUCH HISTORY.
I MEAN--DICK MADE IT INTO A SYMBOL THE WHOLE WORLD KNOWS. JASON GAVE HIS LIFE FOR IT.

FAILING THEM--WHAT THEY FOUGHT SO HARD TO BUILD--THAT'S WHAT WORRIES ME!
I APPRECIATE THAT, TIM. THAT COSTUME WEIGHS A WHOLE LOT MORE THAN ANY SYMBOL SHOULD...

AND I'D BE FAILING YOU IF I EXPECTED YOU TO BEAR THAT WEIGHT.
SO... LET ME KNOW WHAT YOU THINK.

A mask has a double edge, he said. It hides your own anxiety as it strikes fear into your enemy.

A hero doesn't need a mask--
--but it helps.
GENTLEMEN--
IN MEMORY

MEET THE NEW ROBIN!
NEXT ISSUE:
"CHOICES"

Secrets of the New Robin Costume

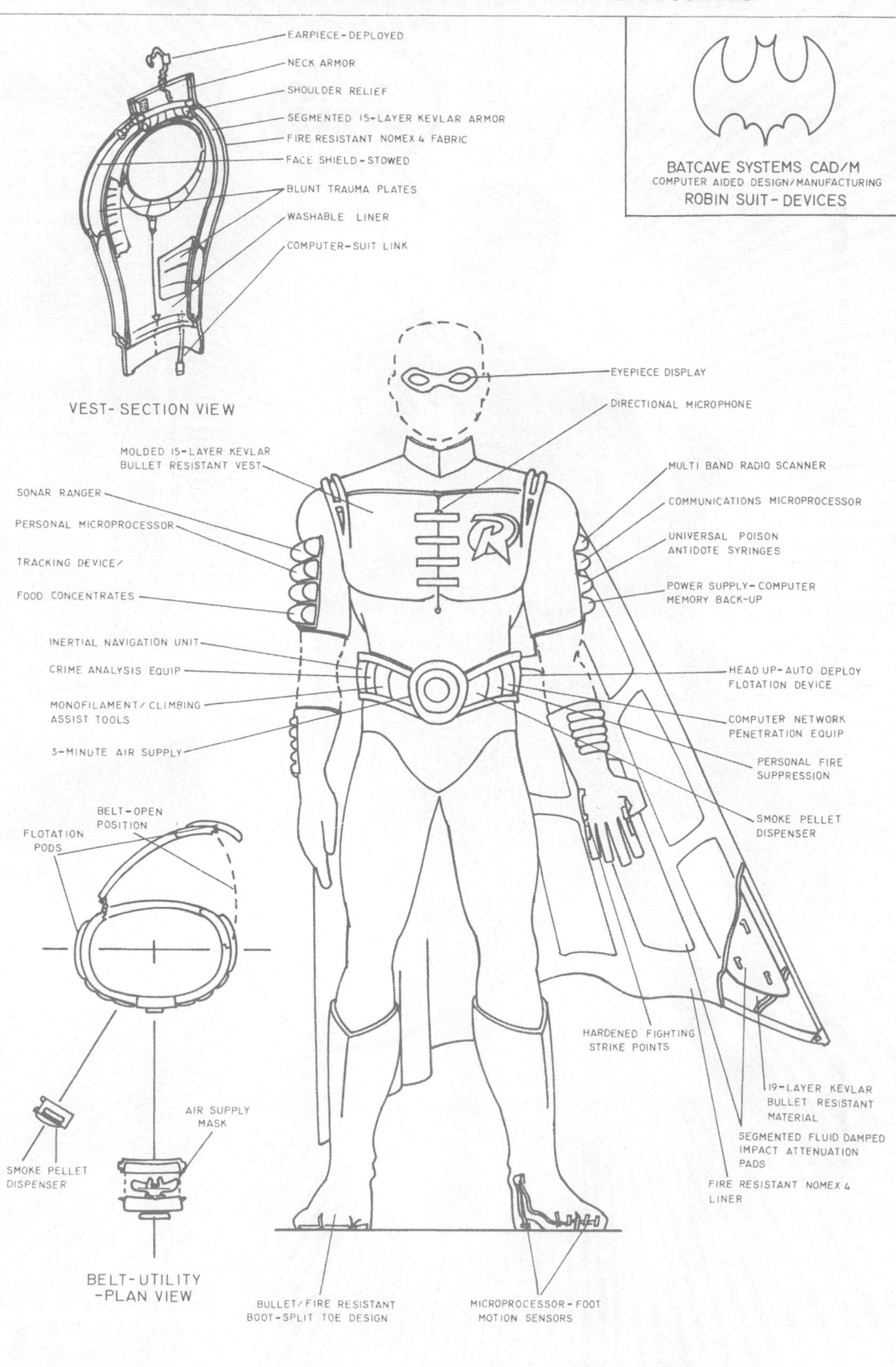

Schematic by Eliot R. Brown

ROBIN

CHUCK DIXON
TOM LYLE
BOB SMITH

THE ADVENTURE BEGINS

APPROVED BY THE COMICS CODE AUTHORITY

Cover art by Brian Bolland

I'VE BEEN WAITING FOR THIS.
I'VE LIVED FOR IT ALL THIS TIME.
I WANT THIS SO BAD.
HOW DOES IT FEEL, TIM?
YOU'VE STOOD THERE THE LONGEST TIME AND HAVEN'T SAID A WORD.
BUT I CAN'T TELL HIM HOW MUCH IT SCARES ME.
BIG BAD WORLD
CHUCK DIXON-WRITER TOM LYLE-PENCILLER BOB SMITH-INKER TIM HARKINS-LETTERER ADRIENNE ROY-COLORIST DAN RASPLER DENNY O'NEIL-EDITORS ·BOB KANE-CHARACTER CREATOR·
IT FEELS RIGHT, BRUCE. BUT I'M NOT SURE... I NEED MORE TIME.
I KEPT THINKING THAT I WAS STILL A LONG WAY FROM THIS.
YOU'RE READY NOW, TIM.
I THOUGHT YOU'D ALREADY DONE ALL YOUR THINKING. I THOUGHT THIS WAS WHAT YOU WANTED, TO BE. MY PARTNER.
WHY ME? WHY DID YOU PICK ME? WHAT MAKES ME THE NEXT GUY TO BE-COME ROBIN?

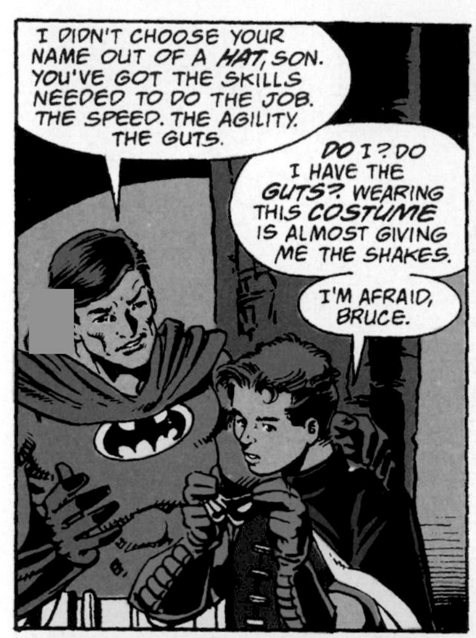
I DIDN'T CHOOSE YOUR NAME OUT OF A HAT, SON. YOU'VE GOT THE SKILLS NEEDED TO DO THE JOB. THE SPEED. THE AGILITY. THE GUTS.
DO I? DO I HAVE THE GUTS? WEARING THIS COSTUME IS ALMOST GIVING ME THE SHAKES.
I'M AFRAID, BRUCE.

I'M NOT SURE I HAVE WHAT IT TAKES. I'M NOT STREET TOUGH.
BUT IT'S NOT THE DANGER OF THE STREETS THAT SCARE ME. I'M SCARED OF LETTING YOU DOWN. I'D RATHER WALK AWAY FROM THIS NOW THAN LET YOU SEE YOU MADE THE WRONG CHOICE.

I DON'T NEED AN IMPULSIVE PARTNER, SOMEONE WHO JUMPS IN WITHOUT CONSIDERING THE CONSEQUENCES. THAT'S NOT WHAT I'M LOOKING FOR, TIM.
GOD KNOWS I DON'T WANT THAT.
THIS JOB TAKES MORE BRAINS THAN ANYTHING ELSE. YOU HAVE THAT. YOU FIRST PROVED THAT BY FIGURING OUT THAT I'M THE BATMAN.

BUT YOU DON'T NEED A COMPUTER HACKER TO SIT HERE AND WORK UP CRIME STATISTICS AND TRACE POLICE RECORDS.
YOU NEED SOMEONE TO WATCH YOUR BACK OUT IN THE STREETS.
YOU CAN BE ALL THAT, TIM...

...YOU JUST NEED THE EDGE.

TOKYO.
YOUR NAME IS SHIVA?
YOU WERE NAMED FOR AN UNSYMPATHETIC DEITY.
I FEAR YOU BRING ME NO GOOD.
I BRING NO ONE GOOD, KOROSHI SAN. BUT I CARRY NO ILL FOR YOU.
I COME TO ASK A QUESTION.
IF IT IS IN MY POWER TO ANSWER, THEN I SHALL. IF IT IS NOT, THEN I APOLOGIZE IN ADVANCE.
ALL THE WORLD ACKNOWLEDGED KOROSHI AS THE MASTER OF EMPTY HAND FIGHTING. FOR TWO DECADES YOU BROUGHT HONOR TO YOUR HOUSE. YOU WERE UNDEFEATED. HUNDREDS DIED AT YOUR HAND.
BUT THEN YOU MET IN COMBAT A MAN WHO CALLS HIMSELF THE KING SNAKE.
I INTENDED TO CHALLENGE YOU FOR YOUR PLACE IN THE WORLD. BUT I FIND THERE IS ANOTHER WHO IS BETTER.
HOW DID HE DEFEAT YOU? WHAT WEAPON BROUGHT YOU LOW?
SONY

THE DARK.
THE KING SNAKE STRIKES FROM THE DARK.

I CANNOT TELL YOU WHERE TO FIND HIM.
THAT'S FINE. I'M GOOD AT FINDING PEOPLE.
I'LL TURN HIM UP, ONE DAY.

MY BODYGUARDS, ARE THEY DEAD?
THEY ARE. I APOLOGIZE IF THAT SADDENS YOU.
NOT THEIR PASSING...
...ONLY THAT THEY WERE OVERPAID.

I HAVE TO LEAVE SO MUCH BEHIND.
I'M TRAVELLING LIGHT-- ONLY TAKING THE ESSENTIALS.
WILL YOU BE WANTING THIS PACKED, MASTER TIM?
UH... GEE, I'M NOT SURE. I...
JUST IN CASE, SIR?
SURE. THROW IT IN.

I'LL PACK MY COMPUTER JUNK WHILE YOU'RE PACKING THE CLOTHES, ALFRED.
EACH TO HIS OWN TALENTS, SIR.
HUH. OBVIOUSLY YOU'VE SEEN ME FOLD CLOTHES BEFORE.

ALFRED, DO YOU THINK I'M MAKING THE RIGHT DECISION BY GOING TO PARIS?
OF COURSE. PARIS IS A WONDERFUL CITY. I'M CERTAIN YOU'LL ENJOY YOUR STAY THERE.
THAT'S NOT WHAT I MEAN. I WONDER IF I'M GOING ABOUT THIS THE RIGHT WAY.

MEANING?
WELL, BRUCE WON'T TELL ME EXACTLY WHAT HE DID TO GAIN EXPERIENCE OUT IN THE BIG BAD WORLD.
MAYBE LEARNING AN OBSCURE TIBETAN MARTIAL ART FROM ITS LAST LIVING MASTER ISN'T WHAT IT'S ABOUT.
YOU MUST DO WHAT YOU THINK IS CORRECT.

MASTER BRUCE WOULD NEVER TELL YOU WHAT TO DO.
TO FOLLOW IN HIS PATH WOULD NOT INSURE THE SAME RESULTS. YOU HAVE TO FIND YOUR OWN WAY. CHOOSE YOUR OWN PATH, MASTER TIM.
EACH EXPERIENCE HAS ITS OWN VALUE. LIFE'S HARDEST LESSONS CAN ONLY BE LEARNED FIRST-HAND.
WHAT DOESN'T KILL ME MAKES ME STRONGER, RIGHT?
A BIT PESSIMISTIC, SIR. A PHILOSOPHY FAVORED BY DULLARDS, IN MY OPINION.
BUT ADVERSITY CAN BUILD CHARACTER.
SPOKEN LIKE A TRUE ENGLISHMAN.
TOUCHE SIR. BUT I BELIEVE THAT MASTER BRUCE CHOSE WELL WHEN HE CHOSE YOU.
JUST AS I KNOW THAT YOU WILL SUCCEED IN YOUR TUTELAGE AND RETURN TO US JUST AS MASTER BRUCE RETURNED MANY YEARS BEFORE.
STRONGER. WISER. AND READY FOR THE MISSION YOU'VE CHOSEN.
MAN. YOU MAKE ME SOUND LIKE A KNIGHT ERRANT SENT OUT ON SOME GLORIOUS QUEST OR HOLY CRUSADE.
I'LL BRING THE LIMOUSINE AROUND FRONT, SIR.

WE LEAVE EARLY FOR THE AIRPORT.
BRUCE IS IN GOTHAM ON BUSINESS. HE'S NOT ONE FOR LONG GOODBYES ANYWAY.
I HAVE A FEW GOODBYES TO MAKE OF MY OWN.
I HATE TO ADMIT IT, BUT THIS IS THE EASIER OF THE TWO.
JANET LYNN DRAKE
LOVING WIFE & MOTHER
AT LEAST I KNOW HER SUFFERING IS OVER.
I CAN'T EVEN KNOW WHAT MY FATHER IS GOING THROUGH.
DAY AFTER DAY, PARALYZED. HE CAN ONLY MOVE HIS EYES.
HIS HAND IS SO SMALL IN MINE.
I REMEMBER WHEN I THOUGHT IT WAS THE BIGGEST HAND IN THE WORLD.
IT'S STRANGE TO BE LEAVING THEM.
SO MANY TIMES THEY TRAVELLED THE WORLD AND LEFT ME BEHIND.
BUT MORE THAN ANYTHING ELSE, THIS JOURNEY IS FOR MY PARENTS.

THE SENSEI I AM GOING TO LEARN UNDER IS A TIBETAN WHO HAD TO GET OUT OF HIS HOME-LAND WHEN THE CHINESE INVADED BACK IN 1950.

RAHUL LAMA IS THE LAST SURVIVING MASTER OF AN EMPTY HAND AND WEAPONS FORM THAT DATES TO THE TIME BEFORE BUDDHA.
THE STORY OF TIBET
HIS ONLY SCHOOL IS IN PARIS.

HIS TEACHINGS INCLUDE MORE THAN JUST FIGHTING--ALSO HEALING ARTS AND MEDITATION.
I GUESS HE IS REVERED BY HIS PEOPLE AS A GREAT MAN AND LIVES IN COMFORTABLE EXILE.

37
I GUESS I GUESSED WRONG.
37 RUE DE CHAMPLAIN.
THIS HAS TO BE A MISTAKE.

HELLO?
UH... BON JOUR?
ANYBODY HOME?

WHO IS THERE?
MY NAME IS TIM DRAKE. I'M LOOKING FOR THE RAHUL LAMA.

YOU'RE THE AMERICAN KID. WE BEEN WAITING FOR YOU.
I AM SHEN CHI, THE NUMBER ONE STUDENT OF LAMA AND HIS GRANDSON. ACTUALLY I AM THE *ONLY* STUDENT.

IS THE LAMA HERE?
SURE. YOU CAN MEET HIM LATER. YOU BRING ANY AMERICAN CIGARETTES WITH YOU?
I DON'T SMOKE.
HUNH.

THIS IS YOURS.
GUESS YOU'RE USED TO BETTER. *MUST* BE, ALL THE MONEY IT COSTS TO LEARN FROM THE RAHUL LAMA. YOUR FOLKS LOADED?
CAN I AT LEAST *CLEAN* THIS?

YOU SURE SPEAK ENGLISH WELL.
I LEARNED IT FROM AMERICAN MOVIES.
I'D NEVER HAVE KNOWN.

WHAT'S IN THE CASE?
A COMPUTER. I BROUGHT ADAPTERS BUT I DON'T SEE AN OUTLET.
YOU *WON'T* EITHER. NO ELECTRIC IN THIS PLACE, BUDDY.
YOU NEED SLEEP ANYWAY. CLASS STARTS EARLY AROUND HERE.

I'LL BE THE ONE SHOWING YOU HOW TO KICK BUTT.
I'LL BE LOOKING FORWARD TO THAT.
THAT WAS GOOD. YOU ALMOST HAD *ME* CONVINCED.

FOR THE NEXT FEW WEEKS I AM THE STUDENT OF THE RAHUL LAMAS.
THE LESSONS LAST FROM FIRST LIGHT UNTIL WAY AFTER DARK.

THE ANCIENT HEALING ART RELIES ON PRESSURE POINTS FOUND ALL OVER THE BODY.
WITHOUT A WORD HE DEMONSTRATES EACH ONE AND HAS ME REPEAT HIS ACTIONS UNTIL I'VE DONE IT RIGHT.

IF THE LAMA EVER GETS TIRED HE NEVER LETS *ME* KNOW IT.
THE LESSONS ARE LONG BUT THEY'RE FASCINATING.
I'M LEARNING HEALING ARTS THAT WERE ANCIENT WHEN ROME WAS BUILT.

WHEN I WAS DONE WITH MY INTRODUCTION TO THE GENTLE TIBETAN ARTS OF MEDICINE, I WAS READY FOR SHEN CHI'S CLASS.
HE WAS HAPPY ABOUT IT, TOO.
TAKE YOUR BEST SHOT, KID. LET'S SEE HOW MUCH YOU DON'T KNOW.

ALL YOU HAVE TO DO IS PUSH ME OUT OF THE CIRCLE. SHOULD BE EASY FOR A SMART BOY LIKE YOU.
UNLESS YOU'RE AFRAID. YOU'RE NOT AFRAID, ARE YOU?

HE'S GIVING ME A CHANCE.
AND I TAKE MY BEST SHOT.
BAD MOVE.

THE TEMPTATION TO SLAM THAT SNEER TO THE BACK OF HIS HEAD TAKES OVER.
UNNH!

ALL OF THOSE PRESSURE POINTS I LEARNED WITH THE LAMA, ALL THE LESSONS SHOWING ME HOW TO SOOTH MUSCLES AND NERVES...

NOW I CAN SEE HOW THEY ARE THE OTHER SIDE OF THE LAMA'S MYSTERY.
THOSE SAME POINTS CAN BRING A MAN DOWN.

I SPENT THE NIGHT USING THE LAMA'S HEALING METHODS TO EASE THE PAIN OF CHI'S CLASSES.

I'M WONDERING NOW ABOUT THE PATH I'VE CHOSEN.

I'M ALONE. I'M TIRED. AND I HURT ALL OVER.

NOT MUCH OF A KNIGHT ERRANT THESE DAYS.

BUT I'M NOT GIVING UP.

A PART OF TRADITIONAL TIBETAN MARTIAL FORMS COMES RIGHT FROM HUNTING. MY ANCESTORS USED THESE WEAPONS TO PUT FOOD ON THE TABLE.

YOU'LL HAVE TO LEARN HOW TO USE ONE OF THESE AS PART OF YOUR LESSONS.

THE NEXT NIGHT CHI TAKES ME OUT TO SEE THE NIGHTLIFE OF THE RIVE GAUCHE.
PIZZA
ARE YOU SURE THIS IS A GOOD IDEA, CHI?
DON'T BE A DOWNER, KID. YOU CAN USE A NIGHT OFF FROM ME KICKING YOUR BUTT.
WHAT DO YOU DO AT HOME FOR FUN?

READ, GO TO THE MOVIES. SOMETIMES I GO TO THE VIDEO ARCADE.
A WILDMAN! LOOK OUT FOR THE PARTY ANIMAL, EVERYONE!
YOU DON'T SEEM VERY SERIOUS FOR A STUDENT OF ANCIENT WISDOM, CHI.

HUH! WHEN THE LAMA KICKS OFF, I'LL BE THE ONLY LIVING MASTER OF HIS FORM.
I'M GOING TO OPEN A CHAIN OF STUDIOS AND RAKE IN THE CASH!
BUT WHAT ABOUT THE HEALING ARTS?
PEOPLE PAY DOCTORS FOR THAT.

ENOUGH OF THIS NOISE! WE'RE GOING TO HAVE SOME FUN!
COME ON, KID!
Club Danger

ISN'T THIS GREAT?
ISN'T THIS GREAT?
HUH?
SURE, GREAT!

YOU ARE AN AMERICAN?
IT'S THAT OBVIOUS?
MAIS OUI. YOUR HAIRCUT. I HAVE AN EYE FOR THINGS LIKE THAT.
YEAH?
WELL, I'M LOSING MY HEARING IN THIS PLACE.
MAYBE YOU WOULD LIKE TO GO SOMEPLACE QUIETER? YOU COULD TELL ME ABOUT AMERICA.
SURE THING. I'D LIKE THAT.
HOLD ON, KID. WHO'S THE GIRLFRIEND? SHE LOOKS LIKE MORE THAN YOU CAN HANDLE.
WE'RE JUST GOING OUTSIDE.
I THINK SHE'D RATHER STAY HERE WITH ME. RIGHT, CHERI?
B.Q.
EEP!
SNAP!
WHAT HAPPENED TO CHI?
NEVER MIND HIM. TELL ME MORE ABOUT THE STATES.

WHAT ARE YOU DOING IN PARIS?
I'M HERE AS A STUDENT. AND TO SEE SOME OF THE WORLD.
AND YOU TRAVEL ALONE?
WELL, YEAH...

NO GIRLFRIENDS TAGGING ALONG? A GUY LIKE YOU MUST HAVE A GIRL.
NO, I... THAT IS...
YOU'RE BLUSHING. THAT'S CUTE.

MAYBE THIS ISN'T A GOOD IDEA. I REALLY SHOULD GO BACK AND LOOK AFTER CHI.
HE'S A BIG BOY. HE CAN TAKE CARE OF HIMSELF.
I'M MORE INTERESTED IN YOU.

NOW HOW ABOUT THAT QUIET PLACE I TALKED ABOUT?
I DON'T THINK...

LING!
LING! WHERE YOU BEEN? I BEEN LOOKING ALL OVER THIS DAMN TOWN. FOR YOU.
JUST HAVING SOME FUN, BILLY. YOU REMEMBER FUN, DON'T YOU?

YOU KNEW I WANTED YOU TO MEET US!
YOU KNEW WHAT WE HAD PLANNED!
OH!

THEY EXCHANGE WORDS IN CANTONESE OR MANDARIN OR BOTH AT MACHINE GUN RATE.
I CAN'T JUST STAND HERE AND WATCH HER GET PUSHED AROUND.
JUST A MINUTE.

DID YOU SPEAK TO ME?
YEAH. LEAVE THE GIRL ALONE. SHE DOESN'T HAVE TO GO WITH YOU IF SHE DOESN'T WANT TO.
REALLY?

I SHOULD HAVE BEEN LOOKING FOR IT.
TOO BUSY TRYING TO FIGURE OUT WHAT TO DO NEXT.
SHOULD HAVE BEEN WATCHING HIS FEET AND HANDS.
UNNH!

I WISH I HAD MORE TIME, WHITE BOY.
MAYBE WE'LL MEET AGAIN.

SHE'S CURSING HIM IN A STEADY STREAM OF CHINESE AND FRENCH AND GOOD OLD ANGLO SAXON.
SHE'S ONE OF THEM. SHE WEARS THEIR COLORS. MAYBE SHE LIKES THAT KIND OF TREATMENT.

BUT MAYBE SHE DOESN'T.

MAYBE I JUST WANT TO FIX BILLY'S TEETH FOR HIM.
MAYBE I'M JUST SICK OF BEING A TOURIST.

BUT I CAN'T FOLLOW ANY FURTHER.
NOT LIKE THIS.
GHOST DRAGONS

SO WHAT DO I DO?
I COULD JUST WALK AWAY.
WHAT WOULD BRUCE DO?

THE LAMA'S SCHOOL IS ONLY A FEW BLOCKS AWAY FROM HERE.
THOSE THUGS SHOULD STILL BE THERE WHEN I GET BACK.

I'M BACK THERE IN TEN MINUTES.
I'M DRESSED AND BACK AT THE WAREHOUSE IN SIDE OF FIVE MINUTES. IT GOES A LOT FASTER OVER THE ROOFTOPS.
THE GIRL MAY ONLY HAVE BEEN SHOWING A BRAVE FRONT FOR THE GUYS.
BUT I KEEP TELLING MYSELF... SHE COULD BE IN REAL DANGER.
R
18

EITHER WAY THIS IS GOOD PRACTICE.
RAHUL LAMA DOESN'T TEACH THE SNEAKY SKILLS.

THE GIRL AND THE OTHERS--ARE A PART OF A GANG. I'LL TRY TO COMPUTER REFERENCE THEM WITH MY PARIS POLICE INDEX LATER.
THEIR ENGLISH IS AS GOOD AS THEIR FRENCH.

SOMEWHERE IN THE BUILDING I'M HEARING THE SOUNDS OF A FIGHT...

OR A BEATING.

I DON'T KNOW THE WHOLE STORY.
I DON'T KNOW WHO'S WHO.
BUT I KNOW I DON'T LIKE THE ODDS.
I'LL EVEN THEM UP A LITTLE.
BUT IT'S GOING TO GET REAL LONELY IF THE GUY I'M RESCUING HAS HAD TOO MUCH.
UNNH!
HE HASN'T.
THERE'S A CHANCE WE'LL LIVE THROUGH THIS.
MY NEW FRIEND LOOKS LIKE HE'S USED TO TAKING CARE OF HIMSELF.

WHERE THE HELL DID YOU COME FROM?
GOTHAM.
NAME'S CLYDE RAWLINS.
NOT TO SOUND UNGRATEFUL, BUT YOU JUST BOUGHT INTO A WHOLE WORLD OF TROUBLE, SON. WHAT'S YOUR NAME.
GHOST DRAGON

CALL ME ROBIN.

UNNH!
ROCKIN' ROBIN, HUH?
NO, JUST ROBIN.
WELL, GET ROCKIN', ROBIN!

THIS ISN'T SCHOOL.
THIS ISN'T A LESSON.

FAIL HERE AND I DON'T GET UP AGAIN.
FAIL HERE AND I DIE.
AND ALL I CAN THINK OF IS THAT I MIGHT LET HIM DOWN.
MIGHT SHOW THE WORLD THAT I REALLY WASN'T WORTHY OF THE HONOR HE GAVE ME.
TO BE CONTINUED

DC
2 OF 5
FEB 91
US $1.00
CAN $1.25
UK 50p
ROBIN
CHUCK DIXON
TOM LYLE
BOB SMITH
APPROVED BY THE COMICS CODE AUTHORITY
BOLLAND
27 BOULANGERIE 27

Cover art by Brian Bolland

THE SHEPARDESS
CHUCK DIXON - WRITER
TOM LYLE - PENCILLER
BOB SMITH - INKER
TIM HARKINS - LETTERER
ADRIENNE ROY - COLORIST
DENNY O'NEIL
DAN RASPLER - EDITORS
THREE WEEKS IN PARIS AND I HAVEN'T BEEN TO THE LOUVRE YET.
I HAVE BEEN LEARNING A SECRET TIBETAN FIGHTING FORM.
AND I'VE BEEN GETTING BEAT UP A LOT.
ALL THIS IS SUPPOSED TO HELP ME BE A BETTER PARTNER FOR BATMAN.
IF I LIVE THROUGH IT.

I'M JUST TRYING TO DO THE RIGHT THING.
I'M AIDING THE OPPRESSED.

PROTECTING THE INNOCENT.

PUNISHING THE WICKED.

BUT IT LOOKS LIKE THE WICKED ARE GOING TO HAVE ME FOR LUNCH.
SO MUCH FOR THE SHINING KNIGHT TO THE RESCUE.

AND I STILL DON'T KNOW WHAT'S GOING ON HERE.
RUN!
UFF!

RUN!
NOW!
UK!
SHE MUST BE PARALYZED WITH FEAR.

AND I'M GOING TO BE JUST PLAIN PARALYZED WHEN THESE GUYS GET THROUGH WITH ME.

GET OFF HIM!
GAAAH!

UGHK!
I SAID OFF!
AAAH!

THAT'S IT, RUN! GO ON BACK TO DORRANCE. TELL HIM I'M COMIN' FOR HIS BUTT!
TELL HIM CLYDE RAWLINS IS GONNA HAVE A PIECE OF HIM!

SHE'S LETTING HIM HAVE IT IN CHINESE AND FRENCH SO FAST THAT I CAN'T FOLLOW IT.
I'VE GOT TO DO SOMETHING.

CAN'T JUST STAND HERE ON MY RUBBER LEGS AND LET HER GET DRAGGED OFF.
NO!
WOAH!
WHERE YOU RUNNIN' TO, SON?
SHE'S IN TROUBLE. WE'VE GOT TO GO AFTER HER.
WE AIN'T GOIN' ANYWHERE. WE AIN'T EVEN...

UNNNHH...
TIME TO AID THE OPPRESSED.
THE WICKED I'LL WORRY ABOUT LATER.

I TRY NOT TO THINK ABOUT THE INNOCENT.

WE'LL GET YOU TO A HOSPITAL. YOU'RE BANGED UP PRETTY GOOD.
NO HOSPITAL. THEY'LL FIND ME.
FIND ME.

THEN I'VE GOT ANOTHER PLACE TO TAKE YOU.
WHERE ?
LET ME WORRY ABOUT THAT. JUST PUT ONE FOOT IN FRONT OF THE OTHER.

HOW DO I LOOK, KID?
JUST GREAT. YOU'RE LOOKING GREAT.
DON'T LIE, KID. I LOOK LIKE HELL AND WE BOTH KNOW IT.
YEAH...

"...BUT YOU SHOULD SEE THE OTHER GUYS."
WHAT I WANT TO KNOW IS SIMPLY, WHY YOU LET HIM GET AWAY?
IT WAS NOT OUR FAULT, SIR EDMUND.

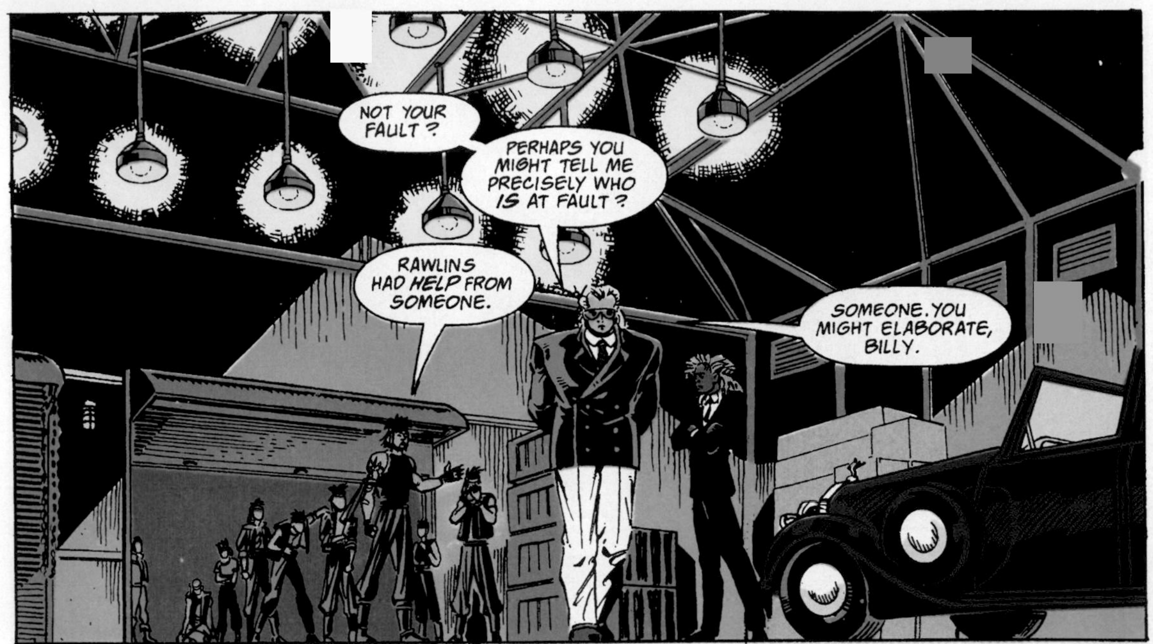
NOT YOUR FAULT?
PERHAPS YOU MIGHT TELL ME PRECISELY WHO *IS* AT FAULT?
RAWLINS HAD *HELP* FROM SOMEONE.
SOMEONE. YOU MIGHT ELABORATE, BILLY.

UH... A BIG GUY. TOUGH. HE HAD A GUN AND TOLD US TO LEAVE RAWLINS ALONE.
YOU DIDN'T *LET* US HAVE GUNS, SIR EDMUND.

GISH

NOW.
WOULD ONE OF YOU CARE TO TELL ME WHAT *ACTUALLY* HAPPENED.
AND BE CONCISE.

IT WAS A BOY.

A BOY?
A YOUNG BOY. ALMOST A CHILD. HE CAME TO RAWLINS' AID. HE WHIPPED THESE GHOST DRAGONS WITH EASE. HE WAS IN A MASK AND FOUGHT WITH GREAT SKILL.

I TOLD BILLY TO REMAIN AND KILL THE AMERICAN AND THE MEDDLING BOY. BUT HE AND THE OTHERS ARE COWARDS.

MOST INFORMATIVE. I SEE I MISPLACED MY TRUST IN BILLY HUE. THE REST OF YOU WILL *NOT* DISAPPOINT ME.
FIND RAWLINS. FIND THE BOY. KILL THEM BOTH.

BOBBO?
YES, SIR EDMUND.
IN ALL THIS EXCITEMENT I'VE QUITE FORGOTTEN WHERE THE ROLLS IS PARKED.
TO YOUR RIGHT, SIR EDMUND. FOUR O'CLOCK.

PERHAPS NEXT TIME WE SHOULD LEAVE THE ENGINE TICKING. THAT WAY I MIGHT *HEAR* WHERE IT IS.
YES, SIR EDMUND.
CAN'T SHOW WEAKNESS BEFORE THE TROOPS, EH?
NO, SIR EDMUND.

SIR EDMUND DORRANCE. BRITISH SUBJECT. FORMER CAPTAIN, ROYAL ARTILLERY.
HONG KONG BUSINESSMAN WORTH BILLIONS.
DORRANCE, E.
FRANCS?
POUNDS.
BUT THAT IS NOT ALL. HE IS ALSO KNOWN AS KING SNAKE. ONE OF THE MOST FEARED MEN IN ASIA. A *GIANT* IN THE HEROIN TRADE.
ENTERTAINING, GENTLEMEN. BUT WHAT DOES THE SÛRETÉ EXPECT A SIMPLE GENTLEMAN FARMER TO DO ABOUT THIS MAN?
YOU ARE A MANHUNTER, DUCARD. ONE OF THE BEST. WE NEED YOUR... INVOLVEMENT.

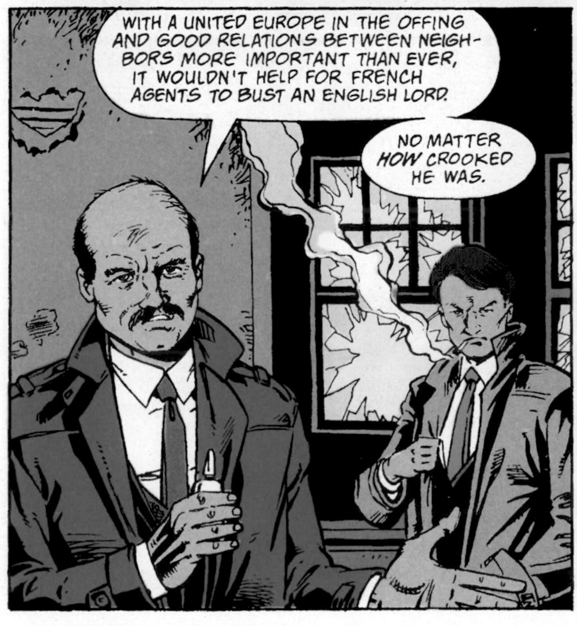

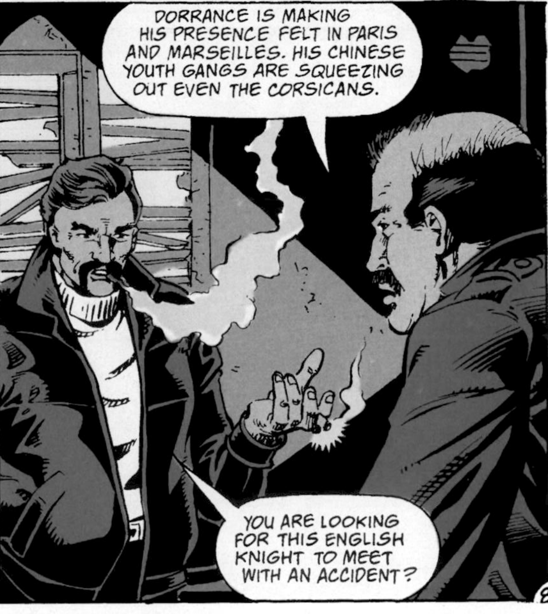

WE WANT HIM DEAD. WE WANT YOU TO FOLLOW HIM WHEN HE LEAVES THE COUNTRY AND SEE THAT HE NEVER RETURNS.
WHAT IS IN THIS FOR ME OTHER THAN NATIONAL PRIDE?
ONE HUNDRED THOUSAND.

POUNDS?
FRANCS.
DOLLARS. OR I LEAVE RIGHT NOW.
DONE.

I START WHEN I RECEIVE HALF OF THE CASH.
THIS MAY HELP YOU. SOME STREET TALK.
DORRANCE'S ENFORCERS, YOUNG THUGS CALLED THE GHOST DRAGONS, WERE SEVERELY BEATEN BY A TALL DARK AMERICAN WITH A YOUNG BOY AIDING HIM.

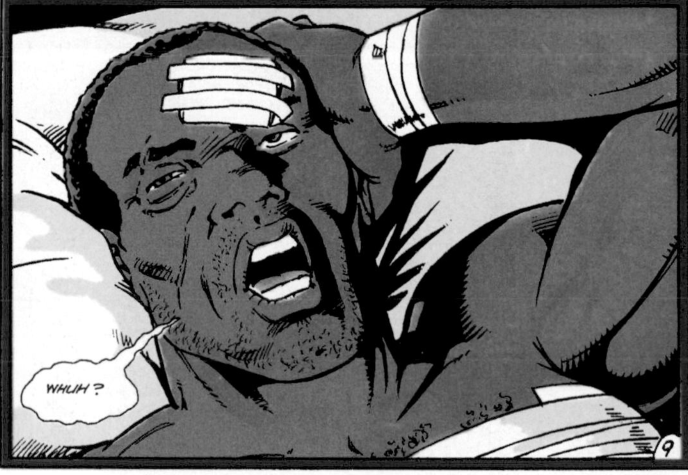
WHUH?
9

MAN. I DIED AND WENT TO HEAVEN.
NOT QUITE. THE HOTEL ST. GERMAIN LOST ITS FIVE STAR RATING LAST SPRING.
HEY KID, WANT TO BRING ME UP TO SPEED HERE?
YOU WERE THE ONE WHO DIDN'T WANT TO GO TO THE HOSPITAL.
PRETTY GOOD TAPE JOB. YOU A BUTTKICKER AND A DOCTOR? THAT WAS YOU IN THE MASK LAST NIGHT?
YEAH. BUT I'M NOT SURE I WANT TO INTRODUCE MYSELF JUST YET. I DON'T KNOW WHO YOU ARE.
MY NAME'S CLYDE RAWLINS.
THAT'S NOT WHAT YOUR PASSPORT SAYS.
I'M A DEA FIELD AGENT. DRUG ENFORCEMENT. I'M WORKING UNDERCOVER.
YOUR DEA CARD EXPIRED THREE MONTHS AGO. YOU'RE REALLY UNDERCOVER.
A DETECTIVE TOO.
SO WHAT'S THE STORY, CLYDE?
I SORT OF HAVEN'T BEEN REPORTING TO WORK FOR A YEAR.
THINGS GOT KIND OF PERSONAL BETWEEN ME AND THE GHOST DRAGONS. THEY HURT SOME PEOPLE CLOSE TO ME.
YOU PROBABLY WOULDN'T UNDERSTAND.
TRY ME.

JUST LET ME GET MY CLOTHES AND I'M OUTTA HERE.
I'M GOING WITH YOU.
NO WAY, KID. NOW WHERE'S MY DAMN CLOTHES?
I TOSSED THEM. I'VE GOT SOME NEW ONES COMING UP.

YOU MUST HAVE A *SOLID* GOLD GOLD CARD, KID.
I CAN TAKE CARE OF MYSELF. WHICH IS MORE THAN I CAN SAY FOR *YOU*.
YOU *NEED* ME, CLYDE.
YOU *BOTH* NEED HELP.
YOU ARE IN DANGER.
NOW WHAT?

DO YOU KNOW HER, CLYDE?

YOU HAVE MUCH TO LEARN OF THE STREETS. IF I COULD FIND YOU, ***OTHERS*** COULD.

THEY ARE ON THEIR WAY NOW.

YOU *SURE* YOU WANT A PART OF THIS, KID?
I THINK IT'S TOO LATE TO CHANGE MY MIND.
WAY TOO LATE.
WE WILL TAKE TO THE ROOFTOPS.
IF YOU CAN'T GO UP, THEN MAYBE *DOWN* WILL BE EASIER.
NO WAY I CAN CLIMB UP THERE. GO FOR IT, KID.

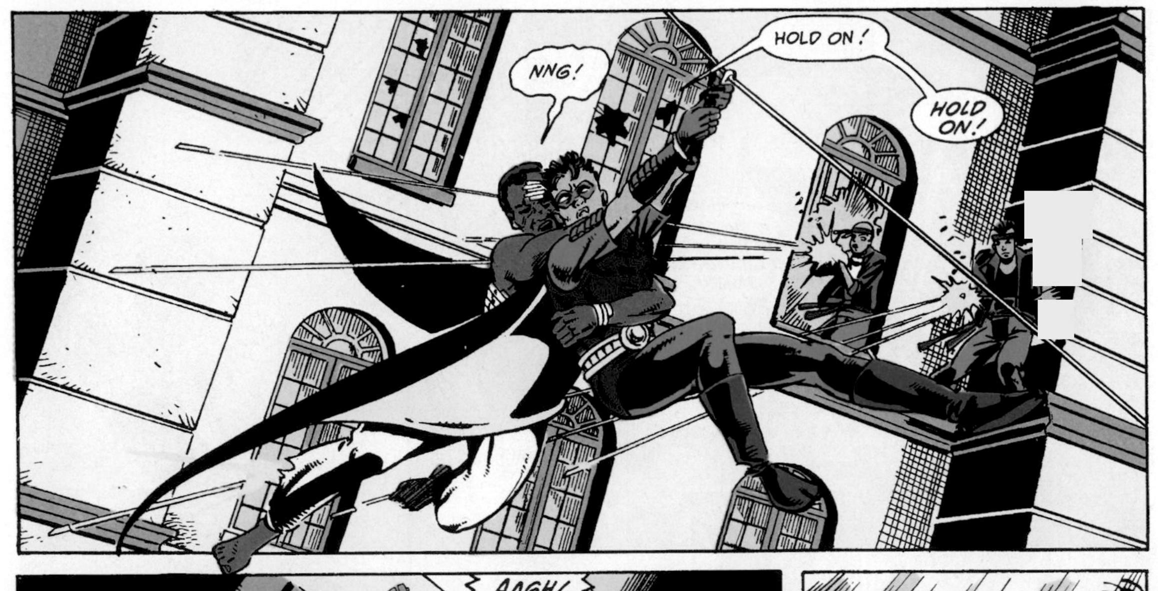
NNG!
HOLD ON!
HOLD ON!

AAGH!

UNNH!
UFF!

CAN YOU MOVE?
DO I HAVE A... UNNH... CHOICE?
NOT REALLY. LET'S GO.

LES FLICS!

POLICE
POLICE
POLICE
POLICE

AGAIN?
YOU BRING ME BAD NEWS AGAIN?

A WOMAN WAS THERE. SHE HELPED THEM.
FIRST IT WAS A BOY. NOW A WOMAN.
I DO NOT LIKE SETBACKS LIKE THIS.
I BROUGHT YOU SCUM UP FROM THE GUTTERS OF HONG KONG AND I HAVE MADE YOUR LIVES VERY COMFORTABLE.

ALL I ASK IN RETURN IS THAT YOU SERVE ME LOYALLY.
PLEASE, SIR EDMUND...

NOT SO MUCH TO ASK, IS IT?
SNAPKT!

IS THAT GIRL I SPOKE TO EARLIER WITH US?
I AM HERE, SIR EDMUND.
STEP FORWARD.

I THINK THERE'S A NEED FOR A CHANGE IN LEADERSHIP IN THE GHOST DRAGONS. I THINK YOU HAVE THE APTITUDE I'M LOOKING FOR.
YOUR NAME?
MY NAME IS LING. BUT I AM CALLED LYNX ON THE STREETS.

LYNX IT IS.
ARE YOU AWARE OF THE MISSION I SET BEFORE THE GHOST DRAGONS BEFORE THE AMERICAN INTERVENED?
BILLY TOLD ME OF AN OLD WEAPON YOU HAD FOUND UNDER THE GROUND. A TERRIBLE KILLING THING MADE BY THE NAZIS.
ANOTHER EXAMPLE OF HIS DISLOYALTY. MY DISCOVERY OF THE KRIEGER LABORATORY WAS TO BE KEPT A SECRET.
I WILL TRUST YOU TO RETRIEVE THE WEAPON AND TRANSPORT IT TO MY COMPLEX IN HONG KONG.
AS YOU WISH.
I HAVE AN APPOINTMENT IN SPAIN. FROM THERE I WILL TRAVEL BACK TO ASIA. YOU WON'T DISAPPOINT ME, LYNX.
NO, SIR EDMUND.

WHEN THIS TASK IS COMPLETED WE WILL FIND THE AMERICAN AND THE BOY.
LEAVE THE BOY TO ME.

"HE IS MY GIFT TO SIR EDMUND. TOUCH HIM AND YOU WILL ENVY OUR POOR DEAD COMRADES."
I DON'T FEEL SO GOOD

YOU SHOULDN'T BE UP. YOU'VE BEEN DELIRIOUS WITH A FEVER FOR TWO DAYS.
HUH. YOU PLAYING THE DOCTOR AGAIN, KID?
WHERE THE HELL ARE WE NOW?

I RENTED US A FARMHOUSE. WE'RE JUST NORTH OF LUXEUIL LES BAINS.
I THOUGHT WE'D LAY UP HERE UNTIL YOU RECOVERED.

THERE'S A CAR OUTSIDE. DID I DRIVE IT?
YEAH. I'M TOO YOUNG, REMEMBER? IT WASN'T EXACTLY A JOYRIDE WITH YOU PASSING OUT EVERY HALF HOUR.
YOU SURE THROW A LOT OF CASH AROUND FOR A KID. THAT COMPUTER DIDN'T COME WITH THE HOUSE, DID IT?
I FIGURED IT MIGHT HELP.

YOU'RE ALL RIGHT. YOU'VE DONE GOOD.
ALL I'VE DONE SO FAR IS RUN AWAY.
SAVED MY SORRY BUTT TWICE NOW. THAT GIVES YOU POINTS IN MY BOOK.

WHAT'S THIS YOU'RE LOOKING UP?
YOU. I ACCESSED YOUR DEA FILE. IT WAS TRICKY. THEY HAD A LOT OF SECURITY CODES.
YOU SHOULDN'T HAVE DONE THAT, KID.

BUT I THOUGHT I COULD...
YOU HAD NO RIGHT, KID. YOU HAD NO RIGHT TO SNOOP AROUND IN MY PAST.
YOU WERE AFTER THE GHOST DRAGONS FOR TWO YEARS. YOU FOLLOWED A TRAIL OF HEROIN AND MURDER FROM MONTREAL TO MARSEILLES TO BANGKOK.

YOU WERE HURTING THEM. YOUR SEIZURES WERE RECORD BREAKERS. YOUR TEAM'S CONVICTION RATE'S NEAR NINETY PERCENT. THEN YOU JUST QUIT.
YOU GAVE UP THE GOOD FIGHT, CLYDE. WHY?

"THE GOOD FIGHT?" THE GOOD FIGHT GOT MY WIFE AND TWO BABY GIRLS KILLED. WHAT'S SO GOOD ABOUT THAT?
AND WHEN I WANTED TO BRING DOWN THE SCUM WHO DID IT, ALL I GOT WAS A LOAD OF BULL ABOUT IMMUNITY.
THE KINGPIN WAS SOME ENGLISH HIGH ROLLER WITH HEAVY CONNECTIONS.

SO I QUIT TO NAIL HIM ON MY OWN. BUT I'M NO CLOSER NOW THAN I WAS A YEAR AGO.
I'M SORRY, I...
YEAH. EVERYBODY'S REAL SORRY. BUT THEY DON'T KNOW WHAT I'M FEELING. HOW I'VE GONE ALL DEAD INSIDE.

YOU THINK YOU'RE ALL ALONE IN THE WORLD?
YOU'RE THE ONLY ONE IN THE WORLD WHO'S SEEN EVERYTHING HE LOVED TAKEN AWAY?

I CAN HELP YOU FIND THE MAN YOU'RE LOOKING FOR. I'VE GOT THE RESOURCES AND EVEN YOU ADMIT I HAVE A TALENT FOR DETECTIVE WORK.
A REGULAR JUNIOR GRADE SHERLOCK HOLMES.
MEMBER IN GOOD STANDING OF THE BAKER STREET IRREGULARS.
HUH.
AND WHAT'S YOUR END OF THIS?
THERE'S THE GIRL THE GHOST DRAGONS ABDUCTED.
BUT EVEN MORE, I WANT YOU TO HELP ME OUT ON MY STREET SMARTS.
SUPERHERO IN TRAINING? GONNA WHIP THE WORLD, KID?
THAT WAS THE GENERAL IDEA. MY MARTIAL ARTS TRAINING GOT KIND OF SIDETRACKED.
I'LL TEACH YOU HOW TO FIGHT. BUT THERE AIN'T NO ART IN IT.
UFFF!
I'M BACK WHERE I STARTED.
NEW TEACHER. NEW MOVES.
SAME OLD PAIN.
COME ON, KID. I'M ALL BANGED UP AND HURTIN' AND I'M STILL WHUPPIN' YOU GOOD.
WHAT YOU GONNA DO WHEN SOMEBODY WHO DON'T LIKE YOU GOES TO CLEAN YOUR CLOCK?

ON THE STREET THERE'RE NO RULES. NO SECOND CHANCES. NO WARNINGS.
GRAVEYARD'S FULL OF NICE GUYS.

NEVER THREATEN, JUST ACT.
JUST KEEP YOUR MIND ON THE GRIEF YOU'RE GONNA GIVE THE OTHER GUY.

LAME, KID.

YOU'RE TOO SOFT FOR THIS, KID.
YOU AIN'T GOT IT.

WANT TO GIVE UP? THINK ANYONE WILL FEEL SORRY FOR YOU?
THIS IS WHERE YOU DIG DOWN INSIDE AND FIND YOUR ANGER, KID.
YOU GOT SOME ANGER, KID?

AGK'H!

unnh!

OH MY GOD.
CLYDE... I... I'M SORRY...
NO APOLOGIES...

YOU'RE GONNA DO ALL RIGHT.

BRAVO.
WHO--?

I'VE SEEN BETTER DISPLAYS OF FIGHTING SKILLS IN SCHOOLYARDS.
YOU NEED SOME ELEGANCE IN YOUR TUTELAGE.
A WOMAN'S TOUCH.
CONTINUED.

DC
3 OF 5
US $1.00
CAN $1.25
MAR 91
UK 50p
ROBIN
TM
CHUCK DIXON
TOM LYLE
BOB SMITH
APPROVED BY THE COMICS CODE AUTHORITY
BOLLAND

Cover art by Brian Bolland

THE DESTROYING ANGEL
CHUCK DIXON-STORY, TOM LYLE-PENCILS BOB SMITH-INKS, TIM HARKINS-LETTERS ADRIENNE ROY-COLORS DENNY O'NEIL and DAN RASPLER-CO-EDITORS BOB KANE-CHARACTER CREATOR
THINGS ARE GOING TOO FAST FOR ME.
I'M IN THE FRENCH COUNTRYSIDE GETTING TRASHED BY A RENEGADE DEA AGENT.
ALL A PART OF MY EDUCATION IN THE MARTIAL ARTS.
HE'S HIDING OUT FROM A CHINESE STREET GANG THAT HE'S TRACKED HALFWAY AROUND THE WORLD.
AND NOW WE HAVE A VISITOR.
WHO THE HELL ARE YOU, LADY?
CALL ME SHIVA.

I AM HERE TO HELP YOU FIND THE MAN YOU SEEK.
SIR EDMUND DORRANCE, THE KING SNAKE.

YOU JUST NATURALLY A HELPFUL PERSON, SHIVA?
WE ALL HAVE OUR REASONS, CLYDE RAWLINS.
YOU SEEK HIM OUT OF SOME QUAINT NEED FOR REVENGE -- TO SOOTH YOUR SOILED HONOR.
THE BOY AIDS YOU SIMPLY FOR THE ADVENTURE OF IT.
CHARMING.

I WANT THE KING SNAKE BECAUSE HE IS RUMORED TO BE THE MOST DANGEROUS MAN ALIVE.
IT'S ONLY FITTING HE MEET THE MOST DANGEROUS WOMAN, NO?

AND YOU ARE QUITE THE DETECTIVE, EH?
I HAVE MET YOUR MENTOR. YOU ARE TO BE HIS LATEST LITTLE ROBIN.
I'M WORKING ON IT.

THERE IS MUCH MORE WORK TO BE DONE. I HAVE INFORMATION ABOUT WHAT SIR EDMUND IS UP TO.
HE HAS SOME PARTICULARLY NASTY PLANS. IT INVOLVES A MAN-MADE PLAGUE.
WE MUST KNOW MORE ABOUT IT IF WE'RE TO DEAL WITH HIM.
WHAT'S THIS "WE" STUFF? YOU DON'T SEEM LIKE MUCH OF A JOINER, HONEY.

WE ALL HAVE OUR TALENTS, ALTHOUGH YOURS ARE NOT OBVIOUS TO ME, RAWLINS. I HAVE INFORMATION THAT ROBIN CAN USE TO UNCOVER KING SNAKE'S MACHINATIONS.
ALSO, CALL ME ANYTHING OTHER THAN MY NAME AGAIN AND I'LL SHOW YOU MY TALENTS.

NOW, WHY DON'T YOU PUT YOURSELF TO USE AND MAKE US ALL SOMETHING TO EAT? NO RED MEAT FOR ME, THANK YOU.
ROBIN, WE'RE LOOKING FOR ANYTHING YOU CAN FIND ON SOMETHING CALLED THE KRIEGER WAR LABS.

SHOOT, WHO LET THE GIRLS IN THE CLUBHOUSE.
MY ONLY REFERENCE LIKE THAT IS TO A GERMAN CHEMIST, HELMUT KRIEGER. HE WORKED FOR THE NAZIS. DISAPPEARED IN 1944.
SOUNDS PROMISING.

THAT'S ALL THERE IS. I'VE SEARCHED THE NEW YORK TIMES FILES AND HACKED INTO NATO DATABANKS.

THERE'S REFERENCE TO KRIEGER ONLY HAVING ONE LAB.
AFTER THE FALL OF FRANCE IN 1940, THEY MOVED HIS FACILITY FROM GERMANY TO FRANCE.
THAT WAY, IF THERE WAS AN ACCIDENT, ONLY FRENCHMEN WOULD DIE. NICE.

RECORDS OF THE EXPERIMENTS THERE WERE NEVER FOUND. NEITHER WAS THE LAB.
WHERE WAS IT?

A LITTLE VILLAGE CALLED AUXILLE.
WE HAD A MICHELIN GUIDE FOR FRANCE HERE SOMEWHERE.
HERE!

NEVER SAY DIE.
AUXILLE IS IN THE EASTERN PART OF FRANCE IN LORRAINE NEAR CREUTZWALD.
IT'S NEAR A SECTION OF THE OLD MAGINOT LINE. CONNECTION, MAYBE? SECRET LAB HIDDEN IN AN ABANDONED FORTRESS?
SUCH A CLEVER BOY.

COME ON, CLYDE, WE'RE GOING FOR A DRIVE.
WHUH? HUH?
ROAD TRIP!

DORRANCE IS MAKING HIS NEXT MOVE EAST OF HERE. WE COULD BE THERE BEFORE MORNING.
IF WE'RE ON THE MONEY THEN WE'LL BE VISITING AN OLD NAZI WAR LAB. COOL, HUH?
OH SURE, REAL COOL, ROBIN.

YOU EVER THINK THIS MYSTERY BABE MIGHT BE WITH DORRANCE?

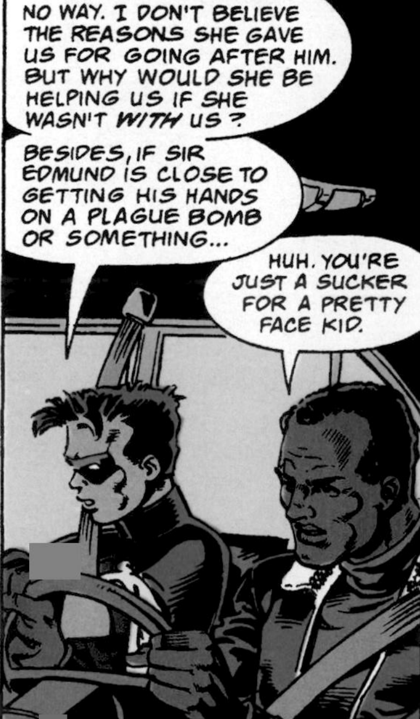
NO WAY. I DON'T BELIEVE THE REASONS SHE GAVE US FOR GOING AFTER HIM. BUT WHY WOULD SHE BE HELPING US IF SHE WASN'T WITH US?
BESIDES, IF SIR EDMUND IS CLOSE TO GETTING HIS HANDS ON A PLAGUE BOMB OR SOMETHING...
HUH. YOU'RE JUST A SUCKER FOR A PRETTY FACE KID.

WELL, I GUESS SHE IS KIND OF BEAUTIFUL...
HA!

...BUT SHE'S KIND OF SCARY TOO.

KRIEGER WORKED ON GAS WARFARE PROJECTS FOR THE NAZIS.
I THOUGHT POISON GASES WERE OUTLAWED BY THE GENEVA CONVENTION.
RIGHT. THAT'S WHY KRIEGER MOVED INTO BIO-WEAPONS.
PLAGUES.
BUT THE LAB WAS NEVER FOUND.
AND YOU AND THE SCARY BABE THINKS YOU KNOW WHERE IT IS.
IT ONLY MAKES SENSE THAT THE GERMANS WOULD USE A SECTION OF THE MAGINOT LINE. SOME OF IT'S BURIED A HALF MILE DOWN WITH ELECTRICITY AND RUNNING WATER.
"THE MAGINOT LINE WAS A CHAIN OF FORTIFICATIONS BUILT JUST WEST OF THE RHINE BY THE FRENCH TO KEEP THE GERMANS FROM EVER INVADING THEM AGAIN."
"IT DIDN'T EVEN SLOW THEM DOWN. NOW IT'S JUST A RELIC."
I SEE LIGHTS DOWN THERE.

I DON'T SEE SIR EDMUND.
HE WOULDN'T GET HIS HANDS DIRTY. THESE SERVANTS WILL LEAD US TO HIM.
THERE'S A *LOT* OF THEM.

MUST BE SOME OTHER WAY DOWN THERE. WE PASSED A LOT OF VENTILATION SHAFTS ON THE WAY UP HERE.
WHAT WOULD THEY WANT WITH A FIFTY-YEAR OLD BIO-WEAPON?
WHY DON'T YOU ASK YOUR GIRLFRIEND? SHE'S GOT ALL THE ANSWERS.
SHIVA.

I FEEL LIKE I'M LIVING OUT A NATIONAL ENQUIRER HEADLINE.
LIKE ELVIS' GHOST IS GONNA POP OUT OF SOMEWHERE.
LOOK AT THIS. I'LL BET IT'S BEEN AGES SINCE ANYONE'S BEEN DOWN HERE.
GOOD REASON TOO. PROBABLY STILL LOTS OF EXPLOSIVES HIDDEN IN THESE TUNNELS.
LIGHTS. THEY'RE UP AHEAD OF US.
WE'D BETTER NOT LOSE THEM. THERE'S THOUSANDS OF MILES OF CORRIDORS DOWN HERE.
ROBIN! GET DOWN!
SUCKER HAS US NAILED. I'M GONNA DRAW HIS FIRE!
CLYDE!
MOVE FAST, KID!

YOW!
CLYDE WAS RIGHT ABOUT THE EXPLOSIVES.
PROBABLY HUNDREDS OF CRATES OF UNSTABLE MINES AND ARTILLERY SHELLS DOWN HERE.

BALLISTIC ARMOR IN MY CLOAK TAKES SOME HITS. MY EARS ARE PROBABLY GOING TO RING FOR DAYS.
BUT I'M ALIVE... FOR NOW.
IT'S THE PUNK FROM PARIS.
LYNX WANTS HIM ALIVE!

LYNX?
WHO'S LYNX?
AND WHAT'S HE GOT AGAINST ME?

LIKE I SAID, THINGS ARE MOVING TOO FAST.

LYNX ISN'T A GUY.

AH. THE LITTLE BIRD.
YOU SHOULD SEE YOUR FACE. IT IS PRICELESS. SUCH A LOOK OF SURPRISE.

I AM NO LONGER THE DAMSEL IN DISTRESS AND YOU ARE NO LONGER THE VALIANT RESCUER.
POOR BROKEN HEART...

UNNH!
POOR LOVESTRUCK FOOL!

I THOUGHT I WOULD HAVE TO FINISH MY ERRANDS FOR THE KING SNAKE BEFORE I GOT TO DEAL WITH YOU, LITTLE MAN.
BUT YOU MADE THINGS CONVENIENT FOR ME.

UGGH!
WHAT WAS THAT?
THE GUNFIRE.
THE EXPLOSION.

SOMETHING WOKE THEM UP.
THE ONLY SOUND IS THE SLAP OF A MILLION LEATHERY WINGS AND THE SCREAMS OF LYNX AND HER HOMEYS.
REAL TOUGH GUYS.
NOW THEY'RE STUPID WITH FEAR.
IT MAKES THEM WEAK AND HELPLESS.
IT CASTS A SHADOW ON THEIR HEARTS.

I CAN SEE WHY BRUCE TOOK ON THIS GIG.
GOOD THING I'VE HAD TIME TO GET USED TO THE LITTLE GUYS.

THEY'RE SPOOKED NOW. IN A HURRY.
FEAR PUT THEM AT A DISADVANTAGE.
GET THE CRATES TO THE TRUCK. THOSE EXPLOSIONS MIGHT DRAW ATTENTION.

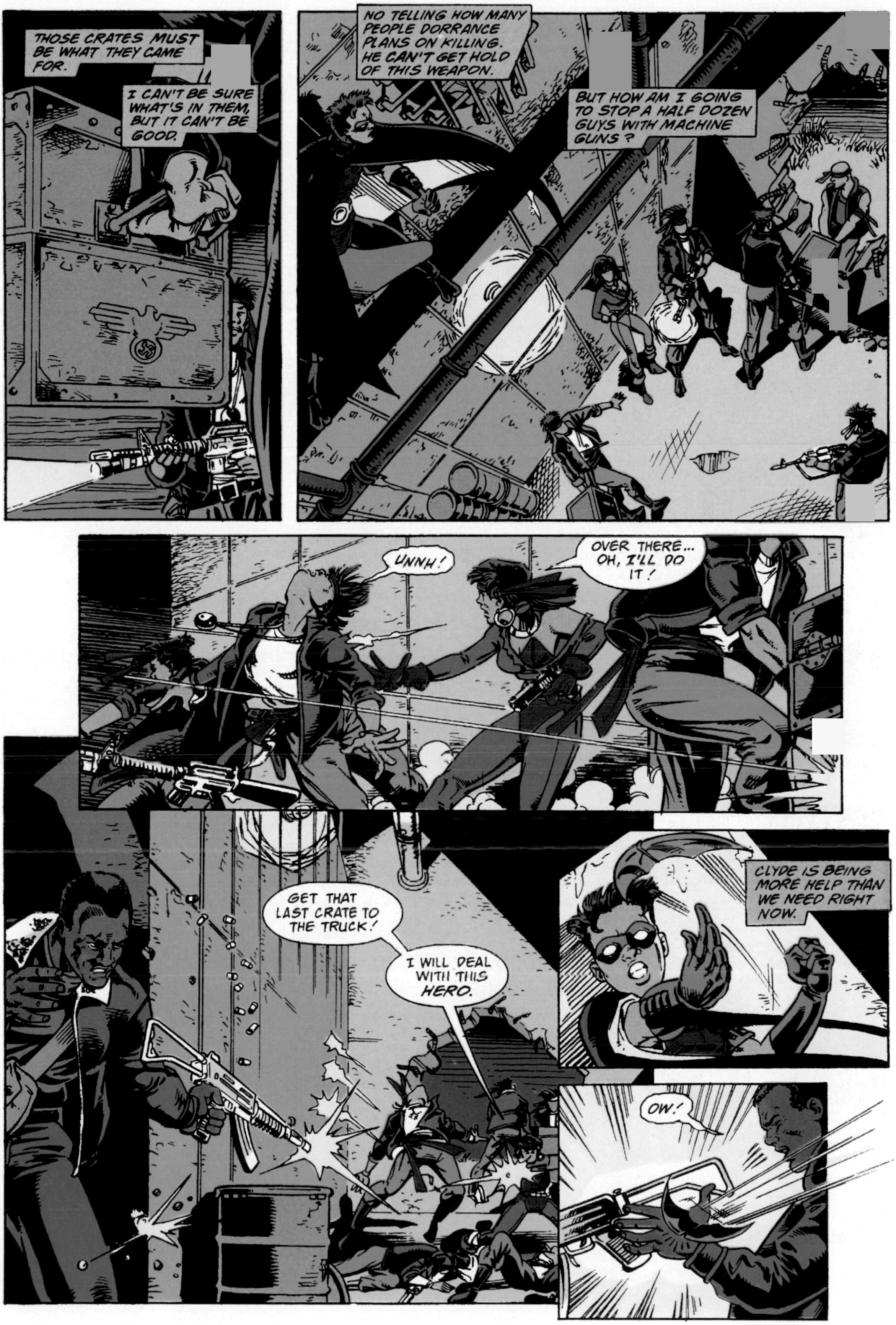

UNNH!

OVER THERE... OH, I'LL DO IT!

GET THAT LAST CRATE TO THE TRUCK!

I WILL DEAL WITH THIS *HERO*.

CLYDE IS BEING MORE HELP THAN WE NEED RIGHT NOW.

OW!

WHAT'S THE IDEA, ROBIN? I HAD HER IN MY SIGHTS.
GUNNING DOWN GIRLS ISN'T MY STYLE, CLYDE CALL ME A GENTLEMAN, I GUESS.

BESIDES, NO TELLING WHAT A FEW HOT SLUGS THROUGH THOSE CRATES MIGHT DO.
UNLESS YOU WANTED TO PLAY NAME THAT PLAGUE?
YEAH...

THE TRUCK IS LEAVING.
WE'LL NEED WHEELS TO FOLLOW IT.!
LAVEZ-MOI

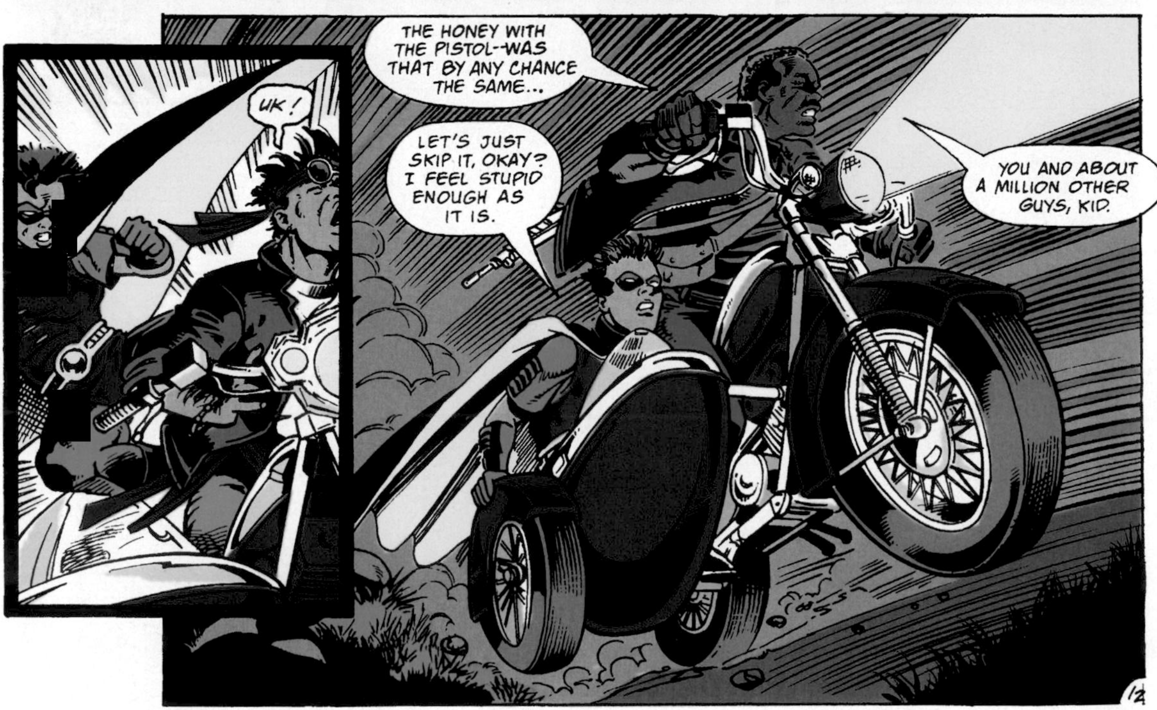
UK!
THE HONEY WITH THE PISTOL--WAS THAT BY ANY CHANCE THE SAME...
LET'S JUST SKIP IT, OKAY? I FEEL STUPID ENOUGH AS IT IS.
YOU AND ABOUT A MILLION OTHER GUYS, KID.

NO GUNS, CLYDE!
TELL THEM THAT!
I'VE GOT SOMETHING LESS DRASTIC.

TELL ME YOU'RE KIDDING.
I'VE BEEN PRACTICING.

AND I USED MY LAST BATARANG ON YOU.

A GLASS MARBLE THE SIZE OF A CHESTNUT.
AAAAH!
IT CONNECTS AT ABOUT 90 MILES PER HOUR.
IT'S NOT LETHAL, BUT IT DOES THE JOB.

A GOOD IDEA WHILE IT LASTED.
BUT NO MATCH FOR A 12-GAUGE AUTOLOADER.
WHOA!

ROBIN!
YOU CAN'T KEEP UP WITH A DANG TRUCK!
OW!

CLYDE, YOU GONNA GET YOUR BUTT KILLED HANGIN' OUT WITH THAT CRAZY WHITEBOY.
DANG RIB'S GONE AGAIN.

SHIVA.
MAYBE SHE IS ON THEIR SIDE LIKE CLYDE SAYS.
I'M LEARNING SOME HARD LESSONS ABOUT THE FAIRER SEX TONIGHT.

I SPRINT CLOSE TO A MILE FOLLOWING THE TRACKS OF SHIVA'S PORSCHE AND THE TRUCK.
I'M TOO LATE.

THE PLAGUE WEAPON IS ON ITS WAY.
SOMEWHERE IN THE WORLD A BUNCH OF PEOPLE ARE LIVING THEIR LAST DAYS BECAUSE I FAILED.

WHEW!
MYSTERY LADY RUN OFF WITH HER FRIENDS... HUH?
I'M NOT SO SURE.
AN AWFUL LOT OF HER "FRIENDS" ARE DEAD.

LOOKS LIKE SHE MIGHT HAVE TRIED TO STOP THEM.
I GAVE IT EVERY EFFORT, LITTLE ROBIN.

MURDER BY DISEASE.
NO ART IN IT. NO SOUL.
SUCH A DECADENT WAY TO KILL.

THEN YOU STOPPED THEM.
ONLY FROM TAKING BOTH CONTAINERS.
THEY LOADED THE OTHER BEFORE I GOT HERE.
WE'LL HAVE TO BURN ALL OF THIS. WHATEVER THIS IS, FIRE WILL KILL IT.

SO SIR EDMUND STILL GETS HIS GERM BOMB.
WE CAN'T GIVE UP, CLYDE. THERE MUST BE A WAY TO CATCH UP WITH HIM.
I HOPE SO. HE OWES ME FOR THE PORSCHE.

THE MOORS BUILT THIS TOWER TO HOUSE THE DEVICE DURING THE TIME THAT THEY RULED SPAIN.
IT IS CLOSE TO A THOUSAND YEARS OLD.

"THE DEVICE DRAWS WATER FROM AN ARTESIAN WELL DUG BY ROMAN LEGION-NAIRES IN THE TIME OF GALBA.

"THE EARTH ITSELF FORCES THE WATER ALONG TWO HUNDRED FEET OF CERAMIC PIPE.

"THE WATER FOLLOWS A PATH THROUGH COPPER BAFFLES TAKING EXACTLY THREE THOUSAND AND SIX HUNDRED SECONDS TO FILL EACH BUCKET IN SEQUENCE.

"AND SO THIS TOWER HAS COUNTED OFF THE SECONDS AND MINUTES AND HOURS WITHOUT FAIL FOR NEAR TEN CENTURIES.
"A MARVEL OF ARAB SCIENCE."

IT IS BASED ON THE SAME PRINCIPLES AS THE GREAT WATER CLOCK IN MOROCCO. IT HAS LOST NOT AN HOUR'S TIME SINCE IT WAS INSTALLED BE-FORE THE COMING OF EL CID.
YOU HAVE LEARNED MUCH OF THE MOORISH CLOCK, SEÑOR.
THAT I HAVE.

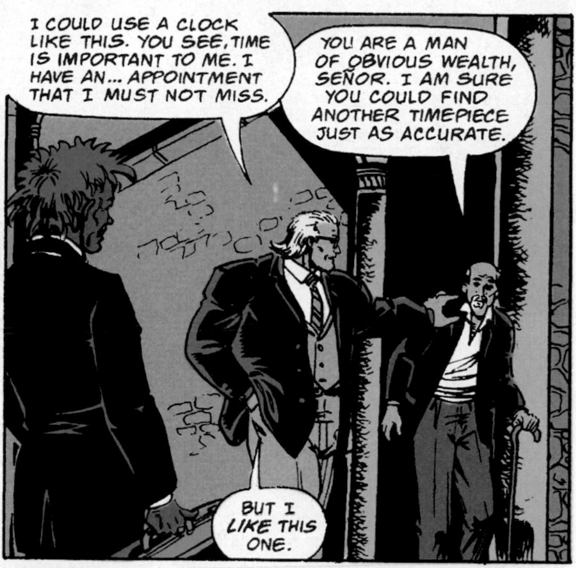
I COULD USE A CLOCK LIKE THIS. YOU SEE, TIME IS IMPORTANT TO ME. I HAVE AN... APPOINTMENT THAT I MUST NOT MISS.
YOU ARE A MAN OF OBVIOUS WEALTH, SEÑOR. I AM SURE YOU COULD FIND ANOTHER TIMEPIECE JUST AS ACCURATE.
BUT I *LIKE* THIS ONE.

THERE IS NEARLY TWO MILLION POUNDS IN VARIOUS EUROPEAN CURRENCIES IN THIS CASE. THE CASE IS YOURS IN RETURN FOR THE CLOCK.
I *CANNOT.* THE CARE OF THIS CLOCK HAS BEEN ENTRUSTED TO MY FAMILY FOR GENERATIONS.

TOPPI, YOU HAVE SIX CHILDREN AND SEVENTEEN GRAND-CHILDREN.
EITHER THIS CLOCK IS MINE OR YOUR FAMILY WILL HAVE SEE ITS *LAST* GENERATION COMPRENDES?

GREED OR FEAR.
THERE IS NO ONE IN ALL THE WORLD WHO WILL NOT BEND TO EITHER ONE, BOBBO.
MOST CERTAINLY, SIR EDMUND.
EXCUSE ME! SIR EDMUND!

WE'RE GOING TO TAKE THIS THING APART, RIGHT?
THAT IS WHAT I HIRED YOU FOR. I UNDERSTOOD THAT YOUR FIRM WAS EXPERT AT THE DISMANTLING OF ANTIQUITIES.
WHERE DO WE SHIP IT?
MY CORPORATE HEADQUARTERS IN HONG KONG. I HAVE PEOPLE THERE READY TO RECONSTRUCT IT.

AND I EXPECT IT TO STILL BE OPERATIONAL WHEN REASSEMBLED.
IT'S INSURED RIGHT?

IS YOUR LIFE INSURED?
UH... YES.
UNLESS YOU WANT YOUR WIFE COLLECTING ON THAT POLICY, I WOULD SUGGEST YOU NOT EVEN CONTEMPLATE DISAPPOINTING ME.
SIR EDMUND, THE PHONE.

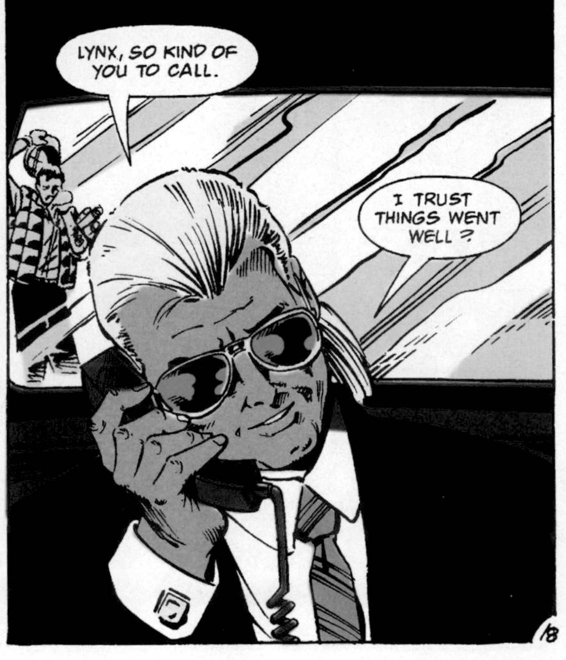
LYNX, SO KIND OF YOU TO CALL.
I TRUST THINGS WENT WELL?

THERE WERE UNAVOIDABLE COMPLICATIONS, SIR EDMUND. OH YES, THE CASES WERE THERE JUST AS YOU SAID THEY WOULD BE.
BUT WE WERE ONLY ABLE TO GET ONE OF THEM.

RAWLINS AND THE BOY ARRIVED. THE BOY I TOLD YOU ABOUT.
WE DEALT WITH THEM AND ARE AIRBORNE NOW.

WHEN YOU SAY THAT YOU DEALT WITH RAWLINS AND HIS PROTÉGÉ, AM I TO ASSUME THAT THEY WILL NO LONGER TROUBLE US, LYNX?

YOU HAVE MY WORD ON THAT, SIR EDMUND.

EXCELLENT, LYNX.
YOU KNOW I DON'T COPE WELL WITH DISAPPOINTMENT.

GOT 'EM!
THE PLANE IS REGISTERED TO BALMORAL INDUSTRIES OUT OF GLASGOW.

BALMORAL IS A HOLDING COMPANY OF TRANG CHEMICAL WHICH IS OWNED BY WORLDWIDE COMMODITIES WHICH HAS GUESS WHO HEADING ITS BOARD?
DORRANCE.
X GETS THE SQUARE.

I'VE GOT A LINE ON THAT PLAGUE.
YOU EVER STOP, KID?

THEY TELL ME THE WICKED NEVER REST EITHER.
JUST SEEMS TO ME THAT YOU'RE AWFUL YOUNG TO BE OBSESSED LIKE THIS.
I HAD THAT PART OF MY LIFE CUT SHORT.
YOU TOO, HUH?
MY MOTHER WAS MURDERED. MY FATHER IS STILL ALIVE... IF YOU CAN CALL IT THAT.
THERE'S A GREAT BIG WORLD OF HURT OUT THERE.
I WONDER WHAT OUR MYSTERY LADY'S STORY IS.
ANYBODY WHO GETS OFF ON MURDER LIKE SHE DOES MUST HAVE ONE HELL OF A TALE TO TELL.
PROBABLY SITTIN' UP THERE IN FIRST CLASS THINKIN' ABOUT HOW SHE'S GONNA KILL YOU AND ME.

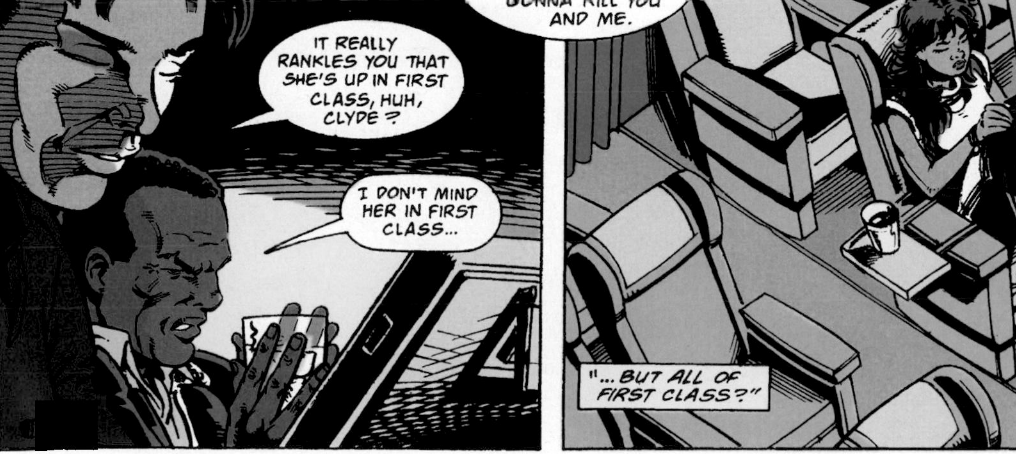
IT REALLY RANKLES YOU THAT SHE'S UP IN FIRST CLASS, HUH, CLYDE?
I DON'T MIND HER IN FIRST CLASS...
"...BUT ALL OF FIRST CLASS?"

YOU CAN REALLY BRING THE WORLD TO YOU WITH THAT THING.
SURE. I ACCESSED FILES OF THE AMERICAN MEDICAL ASSOCIATION WHILE WE WERE WAITING AT ORLY.
ACCESSED? DON'T YOU MEAN *HACKED*?
YOU KNOW MORE ABOUT THIS THAN YOU LET ON.
I STORED THEIR GENERAL FILE ON VIRULENT DISEASES--THE KIND THAT WOULD INTEREST CHEM-BIO WEAPON MAKERS.
I'M USING THIS ENGLISH-GERMAN DICTIONARY I PICKED UP AT A KIOSK IN DIJON TO MATCH UP WITH THE LABEL THAT WAS ON THE CANISTER SHIVA SHOWED ME.

I WAS IN GERMANY TWO YEARS WITH THE ARMY. MAYBE I CAN HELP.
I MIGHT NOT NEED IT. THE LATIN MATCHES UP.
YERSINIA BACILLUS.
NEVER HEARD OF IT.

IT'S GOT A LOT OF NICKNAMES I'M SURE YOU'VE HEARD.
SCOURGE OF EUROPE.
BLACK DEATH.
BUBONIC PLAGUE.

THAT'S WHAT DORRANCE HAS A HOLD OF?
AND HE'S GOT IT RIGHT ON THE DOORSTEP OF THE MOST DENSELY POPULATED COUNTRY ON EARTH.
TO BE CONTINUED!

DC
ROBIN™
4 OF 5
APR 91
US $1.00
CAN $1.25
UK 50p
APPROVED BY THE COMICS CODE AUTHORITY
CHUCK DIXON
TOM LYLE
BOB SMITH
TOPLESS
SHING
NG SHING
LUNG SHING DI
ZHUANG J
CHAN
ACUPUNCTRE
BOLLAND

Cover art by Brian Bolland

STRANGE COMPANY
MY TRIP TO PARIS HAS TURNED INTO A WORLD TOUR.
I'M IN HONG KONG NOW. ACTUALLY, WE'RE OFF HONG KONG ISLAND IN KOWLOON ON THE OTHER SIDE OF VICTORIA HARBOR.
IT'S A WEIRD SITUATION ALL AROUND. BUT SO IS THE COMPANY I'VE BEEN KEEPING THESE DAYS.
THINGS JUST KEEP HAPPENING.
IS THAT THEM?
SHH!
STORY-CHUCK DIXON, PENCILS-TOM LYLE
INKS-BOB SMITH, LETTERS-TIM HARKINS
COLORS-ADRIENNE ROY
DENNY O'NEIL AND DAN RASPLER -CO-EDITORS

A NAZI PLAGUE WEAPON IS ON ITS WAY TO HONG KONG.
WE KNOW HOW. WE HAVE TO FIND OUT WHERE.

SHIVA IS ON THEM BEFORE I CAN MOVE.
UK!
SHE'S NOT ASKING FOR HELP AND DOESN'T NEED IT.

I'M JUST AFRAID SHE'S NOT GOING TO LEAVE ONE OF THEM ALIVE FOR US TO QUESTION.

CLYDE RAWLINS HAS THE BACK DOOR.
HOW 'BOUT WE STAY FOR THE REST OF THE SHOW, LADIES?
SHAK!

HE CAN'T TALK IF HE'S DEAD, SHIVA.
LET'S GIVE HIM A CHANCE, OKAY?
MAYBE HE DOES NOT KNOW ANYTHING.

ONE CHANCE.

WE'RE LOOKING FOR A PLANE COMING IN FOR THE KING SNAKE.
IT WON'T BE LANDING AT KAI TAK. IT'LL BE SOMEPLACE SECRET.
I... I...

IT'S GOOD COP/BAD COP. THIS PUNK PROBABLY KNOWS IT AS WELL AS I DO. BUT HE'S SCARED OF SHIVA.
I'M SCARED OF SHIVA.
IF SHE HAS ANOTHER GO AT YOU I WON'T BE ABLE TO PROTECT YOU.
THE SNAKE HAS A FIELD IN THE NEW TERRITORIES.

TANKA! YOU HAVE BEEN THERE. TELL THEM!
THE FAN-GWAILO MAY GO TO HELL.
THEY WILL KILL US ALL!

NORTH OF SHEUNG SHUI. FIVE KILOMETERS WEST OF THE RAIL SOUTH OF THE SHAO CHAN. IT IS AT THE END OF A FIRE ROAD.
IF YOU'RE LYING WE'LL FIND YOU.

I WILL FIND YOU.

"...THERE'S ABOUT A BILLION OF THEM."

"THAT PILOT MUST BE GOOD TO LAND A PLANE LIKE THAT ON A FIELD THIS SMALL."

THEY HAVE THE CASES CONTAINING THE PLAGUE.

THEY'RE BEING REAL CAREFUL WITH THEM, TOO.

ARE WE GOING TO TAKE THEM OR FOLLOW...

DAMN.

I HAVE TO GET BATMAN TO SHOW ME HOW TO DO THAT.
SHIVA?
LADY SHIVA?

HUSH.
WE FOLLOW THEM. THEY WILL LEAD US TO SIR EDMUND.

I DON'T KNOW WHO SHIVA IS.
I DON'T EVEN KNOW WHAT SHE IS.
I DON'T KNOW WHY SHE'S ON OUR SIDE.

BUT I'M GLAD SHE IS.
THEY UP THERE?
THEY'RE UNLOADING THE PLANE.

WE SHOULD TAKE THEM NOW WHILE WE HAVE THEM.
NO, SHIVA'S RIGHT. LET'S TAG ALONG AND SEE WHERE THIS GOES.

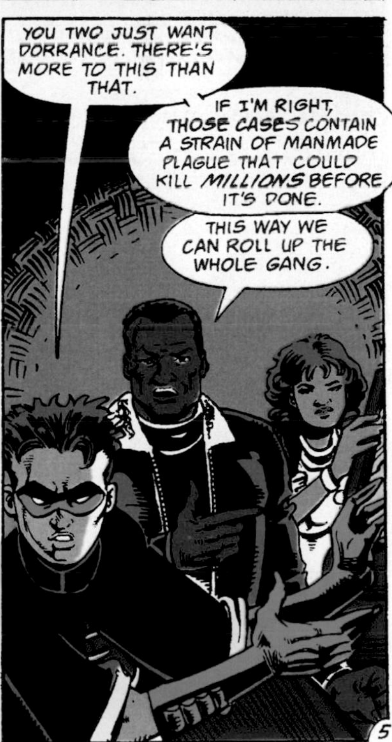
YOU TWO JUST WANT DORRANCE. THERE'S MORE TO THIS THAN THAT.
IF I'M RIGHT, THOSE CASES CONTAIN A STRAIN OF MANMADE PLAGUE THAT COULD KILL MILLIONS BEFORE IT'S DONE.
THIS WAY WE CAN ROLL UP THE WHOLE GANG.

YOU DON'T **CARE**, DO YOU, CLYDE? ALL THIS IS JUST **PAYBACK**. AS LONG AS **YOU** GET TO SIR EDMUND, NOTHING ELSE COUNTS.

THE MAN KILLED MY FAMILY. PAYBACK IS **ALL** I WANT. YOU DON'T UNDERSTAND.

BETTER THAN YOU THINK.

WE'RE GOING TO LOSE THEM.

WE'RE SUPPOSED TO BE THE **GOOD** GUYS. **THEY'RE** MOTIVATED BY REVENGE AND HATRED. WE'RE SUPPOSED TO BE BETTER THAN THAT.

GET IN THE JEEP, KID.

WE FOLLOW THE TRUCKS THROUGH KOWLOON AND BY FERRY OVER TO THE CENTRAL DISTRICT ON HONG KONG ISLAND.
THEY DISAPPEAR INTO A GARAGE AT THE FOOT OF ONE OF THE SKY-SCRAPER BLOCKS.
WHAT IS THIS PLACE? IT LOOKS LIKE A FORTRESS.
THE KING SNAKE'S LAIR. FROM HERE HE MUST RUN HIS EMPIRE. SHIPPING. BANKING. ELECTRONICS.
BUT THAT'S ALL COVER. HIS REAL MONEY COMES FROM THE HEROIN TRADE.
WE'RE GOING TO HAVE TO FIND A WAY IN THERE. IT'LL TAKE TIME.
I HOPE SIR EDMUND DOESN'T HAVE ANY IMMEDIATE PLANS FOR THE PLAGUE BACILLI.
WELL, LOOKS LIKE WE'RE GONNA HAVE TO STRAIN YOUR GOLD CARD AGAIN AND GET US A PLACE TO HOLE UP.
NO NEED FOR THAT. I HAVE A PLACE WE CAN STAY.
A PLACE WHERE WE CAN PREPARE FOR WHAT IS TO COME.

YOU'VE DONE WELL, LYNX.
A DIFFICULT ASSIGNMENT CARRIED OFF IN GOOD FORM.

I DID MY BEST, SIR EDMUND.
I WOULD LIKE TO BELIEVE THAT. I REALLY WOULD.
BUT YOU SEE, THERE'S ONE SMALL DISAPPOINTMENT, ONE NIGGLING DETAIL THAT REFUSES TO GO AWAY.

YOU KNOW I DON'T DEAL WITH DISAPPOINTMENT WELL. YOU KNOW THE MEASURES I TAKE TO PREVENT IT.
BUT A GENTLEMAN CANNOT KILL A LADY. IT'S JUST NOT ON.
SO WHAT AM I TO DO WITH YOU?

I CANNOT LET THIS INDISCRETION GO UNPUNISHED.
BOBBO?
YES, SIR EDMUND.

A PUNISHMENT, BOBBO. NOTHING TOO DIRE. BUT MEMORABLE.
YES, SIR EDMUND.
BE THANKFUL I'VE HAD A PROPER UPBRINGING, LYNX.

AND THINK OF HOW GRAVE THE CONSEQUENCES MIGHT HAVE BEEN.

I'LL BE IN THE ATRIUM, BOBBO. JOIN US THERE LATER, WON'T YOU?

WE'RE STAYING AT AN ESTATE HOUSE ON A HILLSIDE JUST BELOW VICTORIA PEAK.
SOME FRIENDS OF SHIVA'S OWN THE PLACE.
THERE'S NO ONE HERE BUT US.

I GUESS SHE SCARES HER FRIENDS, TOO.
AWAKEN, LITTLE BIRD.
WHUH?

THE TIME HAS COME.
FOR WHAT?
FOR YOU TO ENTER A NEW WORLD.
I-I'M NOT SURE I'M READY FOR THIS.

THERE'S TIME ENOUGH FOR THAT LATER, LITTLE BIRD.
NOW IT IS TIME FOR YOUR LESSON IN MARTIAL SKILLS.

OH.
UH, I'LL BE DRESSED IN A MINUTE.

A WEAPON. YOU WILL NEED ONE TO IMPROVE YOUR REACH.

I'M GOOD WITH A SLING.

FOR CHILDREN. CHOOSE SOMETHING FROM THIS COLLECTION. A GIFT FROM ME.

YOU'RE GENEROUS WITH YOUR FRIENDS' STUFF.

THEY WILL NOT MIND. THEY OWE ME A FAVOR OR TWO.

YOU KNOW WHERE A FEW BODIES ARE BURIED, HUH?

MORE THAN A FEW.

THIS'LL DO. IT COLLAPSES TO FIT UNDER MY CAPE.

A SIMPLE STAFF? IT'S HARDLY A LETHAL WEAPON.

I'M NOT LOOKING FOR LETHAL.

TAK

TIK

TIK

WE WILL BE FACING THE MOST DANGEROUS CRIMINALS IN ASIA. CHOOSE AGAIN.

I WON'T FIGHT MURDERERS BY BECOMING ONE.

I'VE BEEN TAKING NOTHING BUT ABUSE SINCE I LEFT GOTHAM.
I'VE BEEN KICKED AND PUNCHED AND SLAPPED AND STOMPED.
SOME WERE BRUISERS.
SOME WERE EXPERTS.
SOME WERE MECHANICS.
BUT I'VE NEVER BEEN IN A FIGHT WITH AN ARTIST.
NOT UNTIL NOW.

SHE'S FASTER THAN ANYONE I'VE EVER SEEN.
MAYBE FASTER THAN BATMAN.
SHE'S PLAYING WITH ME AND I DON'T LIKE IT.

RED ANGER BOILS UP IN ME.
SHE'S GOING TO KNOW SHE WAS IN A FIGHT.

UFFFF!
SURE SHE IS.

SHE'LL KNOW WHEN SHE WASHES THE BLOOD OFF HER HANDS.
YOU LET YOUR ANGER CONTROL YOU.
ONLY A FOOL THINKS ANGER WILL HELP HIM IN A FIGHT.

THAT WAS A WORLD-CLASS WHUPPIN'.
LESSON ONE IS OVER.
UK... UK... UK.

ALL BELOW ME IS HISTORY. MY PEOPLE TURNED THIS FROM A FISHING VILLAGE INTO ONE OF THE WORLD'S GREAT CENTERS OF COMMERCE IN JUST A CENTURY AND A HALF.
AND SOON IT WILL BE GIVEN AWAY. THE DOWRY OF AN EMPIRE.
THE COMMUNIST CHINESE TAKE IT ALL IN JUST SIX SHORT YEARS.

LIKE GIVING A PRICELESS JEWEL TO AN IDIOT. THEY WON'T KNOW WHAT TO DO WITH HONG KONG.
THEY'LL TURN IT INTO A SPARTAN WASTELAND LIKE EVERYTHING THEY TOUCH. TRAGIC.

BUT I WILL DENY IT TO THEM.
BY THE TIME THEY CLAIM HER, SHE WILL BE A ROTTING CARCASS, FROM LANTAU ISLAND TO THE TOLO CHANNEL.

I WILL NOT LEAVE HER FOR OTHERS TO RAVAGE.
BETTER TO DIE AT THE HANDS OF A LOVER THAN A STRANGER.

BUT WE SHALL BE GONE FROM HERE, SADLY.
I'VE BEEN LONG ENOUGH IN THE ORIENT TO ACCEPT CHANGE WITHOUT REMORSE.

STILL HURTIN', KID?
I'M TRYING NOT TO THINK ABOUT IT.
CARVIN' YOUR NAME IN THAT STICK?
IN A WAY.
YOU'RE STILL A LITTLE TICKED AT ME, AREN'T YOU?
BECAUSE YOU WENT ALONG WITH AN OBVIOUS PSYCHOPATH'S DECISION TO ENDANGER THE LIVES OF MILLIONS OF INNOCENTS?
YOU'RE JUST BEING SENSITIVE, CLYDE.
DORRANCE KILLED EVERYTHING I EVER LOVED. EXCUSE ME IF I CAN'T WORK UP A LOT OF COMPASSION FOR A BUNCHA STRANGERS.
I KNOW WHO YOU ARE. BOY WONDER TO THAT FREAK IN GOTHAM. SO DON'T JUDGE ME, ROBIN.
YOU GOT THIS ALL BACKWARDS.
GETTING BACK THAT BIO-WEAPON WAS THE MOST IMPORTANT THING. DORRANCE WAS OUR SECOND PRIORITY. WE COULD HAVE TAKEN HIM LATER.
BUT NOW YOU AND LADY SCHIZO HAVE PUT A RUSH ON BOTH.

ROLAND SECURITY LIMITED INSTALLED ALL OF DORRANCE'S SECURITY SYSTEMS.
HOW DO YOU KNOW THAT?
I CALLED THE CONTRACTOR WHO BUILT THE PLACE.
YASS, ROLAND SECURITY SALES? THIS IS LORD REGINALD SMYTHE CARRINGTON. YOU WERE RECOMMENDED TO ME BY MY DEAR FRIEND SIR EDMUND DORRANCE.
HE TOLD ME THAT YOU PREPARED HIS SECURITY SYSTEMS.
WE DID, LORD REGINALD.
WELL, I SHOULD LIKE THE SAME SYSTEM FOR MY NEW BUSINESS COMPLEX. WHAT SORT OF THINGS WOULD I BE LOOKING FOR?
I HAVE THE DORRANCE ACCOUNT RIGHT HERE.
SONICS AND MOTION DETECTORS ON THE GROUND FLOOR.
SPLENDID.
VIDEO CAMERAS AND SEISMICS ON THE ROOFTOP.
DO GO ON.
INFRA RED SCANNERS IN THE GARAGE APPROACHES.
SMASHING.
VIDEO & SEISMIC
PENTHOUSE
52 FLOO
32ND FLOOR
17th FLOOR
SMASHING?
I'M GETTING THE *INFORMATION*, AREN'T I?
LORD REGINALD? HELLO?

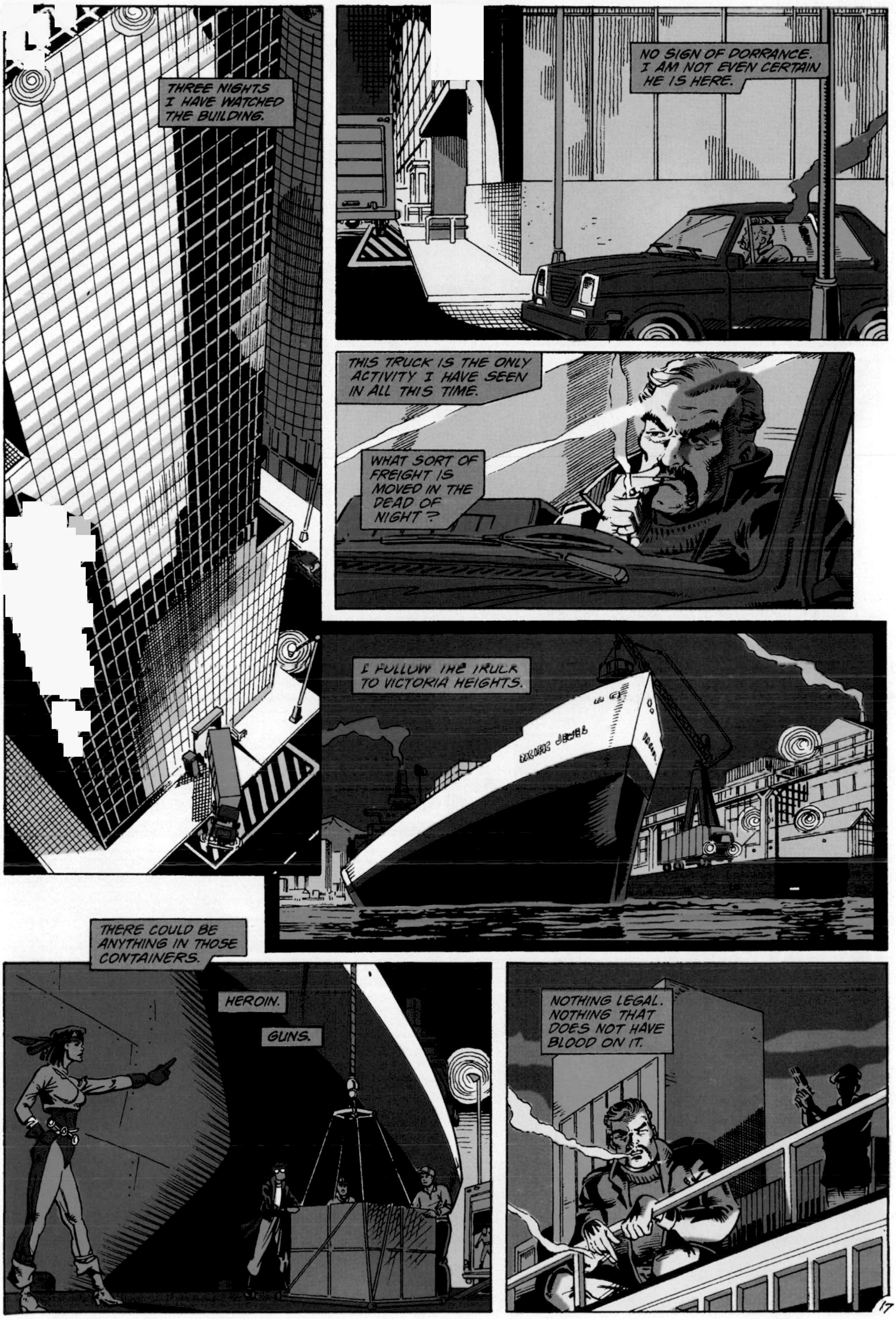

THREE NIGHTS I HAVE WATCHED THE BUILDING.

NO SIGN OF DORRANCE. I AM NOT EVEN CERTAIN HE IS HERE.

THIS TRUCK IS THE ONLY ACTIVITY I HAVE SEEN IN ALL THIS TIME.

WHAT SORT OF FREIGHT IS MOVED IN THE DEAD OF NIGHT?

I FOLLOW THE TRUCK TO VICTORIA HEIGHTS.

THERE COULD BE ANYTHING IN THOSE CONTAINERS.

PLEASE TURN SLOWLY, SIR.
I AM A TOURIST. I ONLY WANTED TO SEE THE SHIP.
ARE YOU ARMED, SIR?
THANK YOU, SIR.
WOULD YOU PLEASE COME WITH US, SIR?
I HAVE LITTLE CHOICE.
A TRIP TO THE LOCAL POLICE HEADQUARTERS, A CALL TO INTERPOL AND I WILL BE RELEASED.
THEN THE HUNT FOR DORRANCE RESUMES.

POLICE

YOU ARE NOTHING.
YOU ARE LESS THAN NOTHING.
YOU ARE A CHILD.
THAT IS HOW YOUR OPPONENTS MUST SEE YOU. THEY WILL UNDERESTIMATE YOUR SKILLS BECAUSE OF YOUR AGE AND SIZE
THAT IS YOUR ADVANTAGE.
BUT YOU MUST NEVER SEE YOURSELF THAT WAY.
DRAW THEM TO ATTACK. FEIGN WEAKNESS. FEIGN FEAR.
AND STRIKE WHEN THEY ARE CLOSE.
HERE'S THE PATTERN.
SHE'LL LET ME MAKE ONE MOVE.
I'VE GOT TO MAKE IT A GOOD ONE.

THE WHISTLING STAFF DISTRACTS HER.

FOR JUST AN INSTANT SHE STEPS INTO MY ARC.

HOW DOES THE WORK PROCEED, BOBBO.
MOST EXCELLENTLY, SIR EDMUND. THE WORKERS ARE NEARLY FINISHED WITH YOUR CLOCK.
THE TRICKLE OF WATER WILL BE A WELCOME ADDITION TO THE SOUNDS FROM THE ATRIUM.

WE WILL INSTALL THE BIO-WEAPON IN ONE OF THE CLOCK'S HOUR RECEPTACLES. THE PLAGUE AGENT WILL BE ENCASED IN A BLOCK OF SALT.
THE CONTAINER WILL FILL IN TWELVE HOURS. THE SALT WILL TAKE ANOTHER THREE TO MELT.

THE SCOURGE WILL BE AIRBORNE AND DISPERSED THROUGH OUR VENTILATION SYSTEM TO FALL ON THE CITY.
THERE IN THE STINKING ALLEYS AND MISERABLE HOVELS IT MAY BREED.

SOUR GRAPES INDEED FOR OUR MAINLAND FRIENDS.
BUT WE SHALL BE LONG GONE BY THAT TIME.
TO BE CONCLUDED

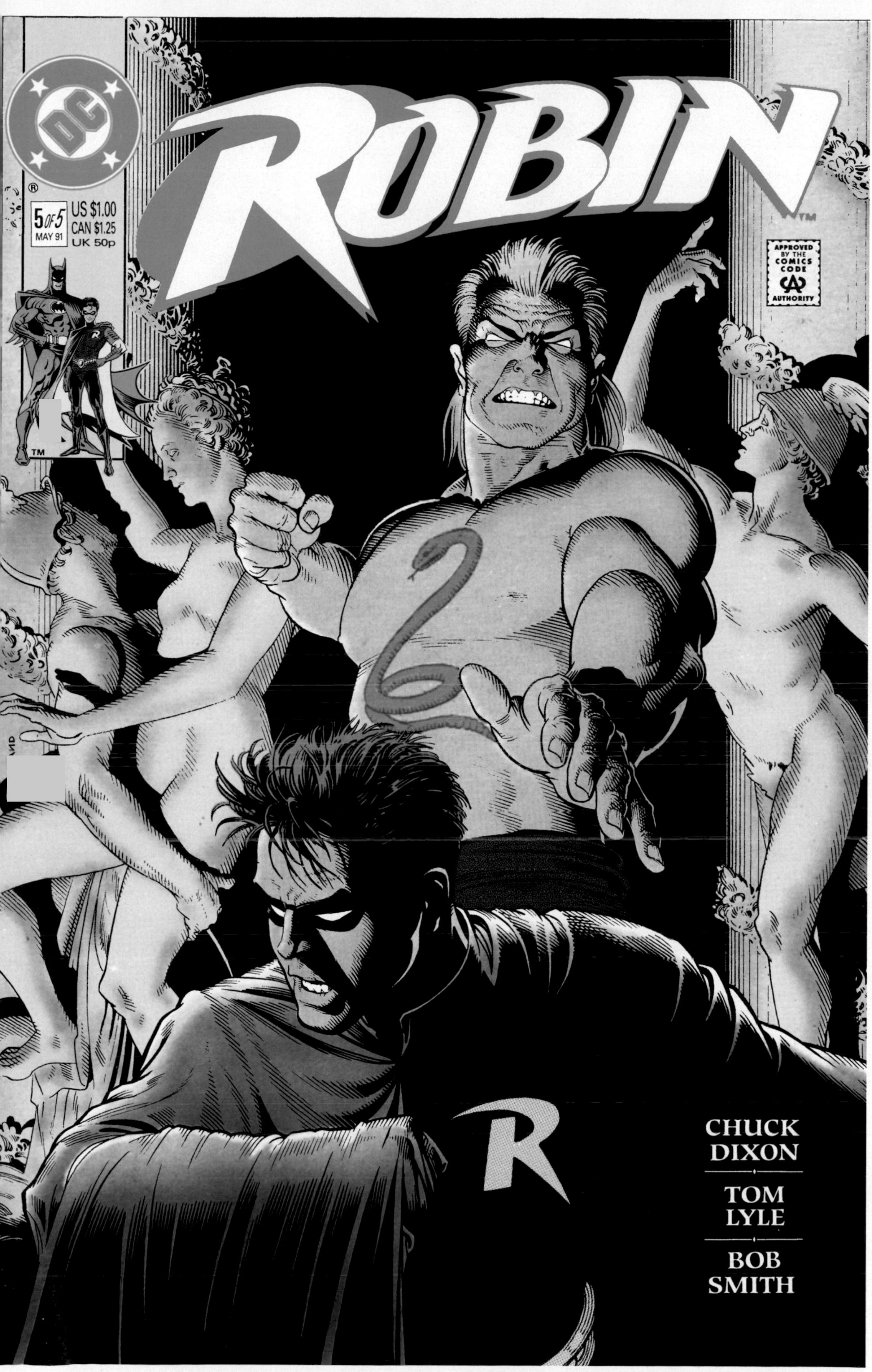
ROBIN
5 OF 5
MAY 91
US $1.00
CAN $1.25
UK 50p
APPROVED BY THE COMICS CODE AUTHORITY
CHUCK DIXON
TOM LYLE
BOB SMITH

Cover art by Brian Bolland

THE DARK
STORY - CHUCK DIXON
PENCILS - TOM LYLE
INKS - BOB SMITH
LETTERS - TIM HARKINS
COLORS - ADRIENNE ROY
CO-EDITS - DENNY O'NEIL
DAN RASPLER
CHARACTER CREATED BY BOB KANE.
THIS IS THE HOUSE THAT EVIL BUILT.
THE DORRANCE BUILDING.
A SHINY GLASS TOWER THAT MASKS AN EMPIRE BUILT ON MISFORTUNE, WEAKNESS AND DEATH.
THE SLOW DEATH THAT HEROIN BRINGS.

BUT SIR EDMUND DORRANCE HAD HIS HANDS ON SOMETHING EVEN DEADLIER THAN THE WHITE POWDER REFINED IN HIS LABS IN BANGKOK.

HE'S GOT A LITTLE PIECE OF HORROR LEFT OVER FROM THE NAZIS.
I'VE FOLLOWED HIM ACROSS THE WORLD FROM PARIS TO HONG KONG.

I'M SUPPOSED TO BE LEARNING TO TAKE CARE OF MYSELF ON THE STREETS...

...NOT SAVING THE WORLD FROM ONE OF HITLER'S PET PLAGUE PROJECTS.

WHAT CAN YOU SEE?
I CAN ONLY GUESS. BUT IT LOOKS LIKE THEY HAVE THE BIO-WEAPON DOWN THERE.
IT'S GOT SOMETHING TO DO WITH THAT CRAZY FOUNTAIN THEY HAVE IN THE LOBBY.

HOW ARE WE PROCEEDING, BOBBO?
MOST EXCELLENTLY, SIR EDMUND.
THE CONTAMINANT IS NEARLY IN PLACE, SIR EDMUND.
EACH HOUR WILL DIVERT A HALF LITER OF WATER FROM THE CLOCK TO THIS CYLINDER.
IN A WEEK'S TIME THE LEVEL WILL HAVE RISEN TO THE SALT BLOCK.
THEN TWELVE HOURS FOR THE SALT TO MELT INTO A SALT SOLUTION, THE PERFECT BREEDING GROUND FOR THOSE NASTY MICROBES.
MORE THAN ENOUGH TIME TO WRAP UP AFFAIRS HERE AND MOVE ON.
SEVEN AND A HALF DAYS.
THEN WE MAKE OUR FORTUNE IN AMERICA.
WE HAVE TO MOVE IN SOON. IT LOOKS LIKE THEY'RE GOING TO USE THAT FOUNTAIN TO TRIGGER THE PLAGUE WEAPON.
AND I DOUBT SIR EDMUND WILL BE HERE WHEN THAT HAPPENS.

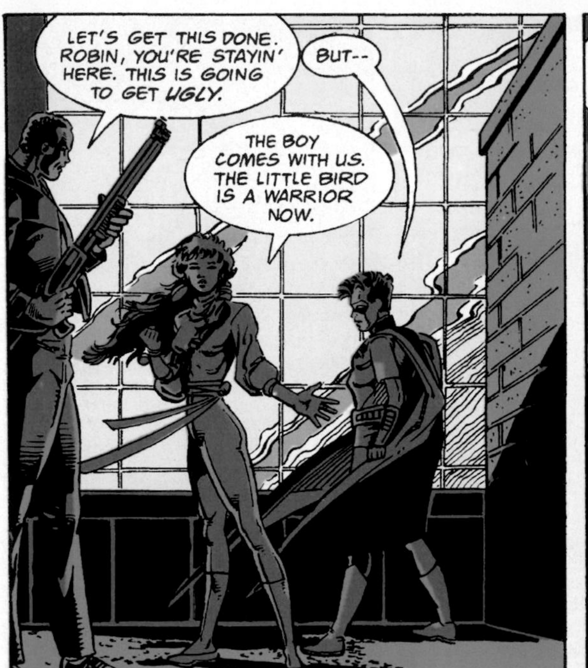

I WANT HIM OUT OF IT!

YOU PLAY YOUR SICK LITTLE GAMES ON YOUR TIME, LADY. I'M GOING AFTER DORRANCE NOW.

RIGHT NOW.

CLYDE! WAIT!

LET HIM GO.

HE IS ALREADY A DEAD MAN. CAN'T YOU SEE IT IN HIS FACE?

HE DIED WITH HIS FAMILY.

BUT WE CAN'T LET HIM GO ALONE, SHIVA. IF SIR EDMUND IS ALL YOU SAY HE IS, THEN CLYDE DOESN'T STAND A CHANCE.
SHIVA?

AW...
NOT AGAIN.!

I'VE REVIEWED THE SCHEMATICS OF THE BUILDING'S SECURITY SYSTEMS SO THAT I KNOW THEM BY HEART.
I JUST HAVE TO HOPE DORRANCE HASN'T HAD ANY NEW STUFF PUT IN I DON'T KNOW ABOUT.

THE LEAST RISKY WAY IN IS FROM UNDERNEATH.

NO TIME FOR TRICKY STUFF.
MOST OF THE SYSTEM IS IN-HOUSE. NO REASON DORRANCE WOULD WANT THE LAW CALLED IN.

HE'S ALREADY GOT A PRIVATE ARMY OF SECURITY GUYS ON SITE.
FIRST I CUT THE SONICS ON GROUND LEVEL.

JUST HAVE TO HOPE...

... CLYDE HASN'T...
PING

... TRIPPED THEM YET...

HE WON'T GET VERY FAR SHOOTING HIS WAY INTO THE BUILDING.
IF SIR EDMUND IS WHERE WE THINK HE IS, THEN WE'VE GOT TO SNEAK UP FIFTY FLOORS.

NO GUNSHOTS.
WE'RE STILL ON SNEAKY TIME.
JUST TAKE THIS A FLOOR AT A TIME.
HEY!
IT'S NOT GOING TO WORK OUT THAT WAY.

THERE'S LOTS OF THESE GUYS.

DORRANCE MUST GET A DEAL ON THEM BY THE DOZEN.

HE BUYS THEM LOTS OF BULLETS TOO.

LOSING TIME. GOT TO GET TO THE PLAGUE WEAPON FIRST.
CLYDE IS GOING TO HAVE TO LOOK OUT FOR HIMSELF FOR A WHILE.

I CAN ONLY HOPE THAT MAYBE DORRANCE ISN'T EVEN IN THE BUILDING.
DORRANCE?
YOU UP HERE?
MAYBE THE KING SNAKE HAS SLITHERED AWAY UNDER A NEW ROCK.
I HOPE SO. RAWLINS IS STREET TOUGH, SURE.
I'M COMIN' FOR YOU, DORRANCE. HIDING AIN'T GOING TO HELP YOU.
NOT ONE BIT.
BUT SHIVA SAID SIR EDMUND IS THE MOST DANGEROUS MAN IN THE WORLD.
MOST DANGEROUS MAN, SHE SAYS.
YOU'RE GOING TO HAVE TO STEP OUT HERE AND DEAL WITH ME, SUCKER.

HE IS NOWHERE TO BE FOUND.
STUPID! YOU ARE *ALL* STUPID! TO LET A *CHILD* GET AWAY FROM YOU.
THAT *SOUND!*
SPISH!
HE WAS HERE. HE WAS HERE *SECONDS* AGO.
HE STUMBLED HERE, SPILLED THOSE BOLTS.

COME ON OUT, SCUM. LET'S GET THIS OVER WITH.
IT IS OVER ALREADY.
UNNNH!
YOU ARE A SEEKER OF VENGEANCE.
I HAVE WRONGED YOU. HURT YOU. AND NOW YOU SEEK JUSTICE.
UFF!
WHERE IS THE STRENGTH OF THE RIGHTEOUS?
WHERE IS THE WRATH OF THE AVENGER?
LET ME HELP YOU FIND IT.
I WILL TELL YOU HOW YOUR FAMILY DIED.
10

HE CAME THIS WAY.
BRING HIM OUT INTO THE OPEN. I WANT A CLEAR SHOT.

WAIT! THERE HE IS!
IN THE CLOCK!

I'M NOT SURE I'M DOING THE RIGHT THING.
HOW DOES THIS GADGET FIGURE IN TRIGGERING THE PLAGUE WEAPON?
BLAM

BLAM
THEY'VE GOT THE PLAGUE ENCASED IN SOME KIND OF CRYSTAL STUFF.
THE WATER HAS TO HAVE SOMETHING TO DO WITH IT.

WHAT ARE YOU DOING? IF A STRAY SHOT SHOULD BREAK THE SALT BLOCK THAT ENCLOSES THE CONTAMINANT, WE COULD ALL BE EXPOSED.
YOU WOULD RELEASE THE PLAGUE!
STRAY SHOT? I NEVER MISS!

THE CHILDREN DIED IN THEIR SLEEP. BUT YOUR WIFE... SHE DIED SCREAMING YOUR NAME.
YOU... YOU...

I'LL KILL YOU!

I SERIOUSLY DOUBT THAT.

I ONLY WISH I COULD SEE YOU DIE.

HERE IS YOUR STRAY SHOT, MY FRIEND.
UGKH!
BLAM

NOW, BACK TO THE HUNT.

I COULD TAKE HIM IN THE HEAD.
I COULD TRY FOR HIS TRIGGER HAND.

BUT I'VE GOT TO TAKE OUT THAT CANNON HE'S FIRING.

CENTER SHOT.

AAAAAAAAAAAA

THE BIO-WEAPON IS SAFE FOR NOW. BOBBO MADE SURE NO WATER IS GOING TO GET NEAR IT.
AND HE MANAGED TO CHASE ALL OF THE GUARDS OFF.

SO THERE SHOULD BE NOTHING BETWEEN ME AND CLYDE.

ONLY THE MOST DANGEROUS MAN IN THE WORLD.

ONLY THE MOONLIGHT TO SEE BY.
SIR EDMUND'S BLINDNESS WON'T BE A HANDICAP HERE.

I'M TOO LATE.

DORRANCE IS HERE.

I CAN FEEL HIM.

SO YOU *ARE* ALONE.

I KNOW BETTER THAN TO ANSWER.

NO SIGN OF YOUR BAT-WINGED ELDER.

HE WANTS MY VOICE. TO DISTRACT ME.

TO FIND ME.

I GET THE FIRST STRIKE.
MUSIC?

HE'S FAST.
THE MISS IS ONLY BY INCHES.
YOU ATTACK ME WITH A TOY?

HE KNOWS THIS ROOM.
HE CAN PLACE ME WITHOUT SEEING ME.

MY BREATH IS GONE.
I FEEL A RIB GOING.

GOT TO STAY OUT OF HIS REACH.
CAN'T TAKE ANOTHER HIT LIKE THAT.
YOU ARE BATMAN'S PRODIGY?
YOU'RE NOTHING BUT AN UPSTART.
A DELUDED INNOCENT.

MORE MUSIC.
A DEATH SONG.

I AM NOT WITHOUT PITY, BOY.

I'LL MAKE YOUR END A QUICK ONE.

UH?
HIS SURPRISE ONLY GIVES ME AN INSTANT OF HESITATION.

I PUT EVERYTHING INTO IT.

UNNNH!

NO.

NOOOOOOOO
FIFTY STORIES IS A LONG WAY TO FALL.

MY SIDE IS ON FIRE WHERE SIR EDMUND KICKED ME.
EVERY STEP IS PAINFUL.

SO, YOU MET THE KING SNAKE IN HIS LAIR AND LIVED.
WHO THE HECK ARE YOU ?
I'M ON THE SIDE OF THE ANGELS, FOR NOW. IS DORRANCE DEAD ?

HE'S DEAD. TOTALLY.
I HAVE CALLED IN THE PROPER AUTHORITIES. THEY SHOULD BE HERE AT ANY TIME.
THERE'S A REAL DANGEROUS GERM WARFARE WEAPON HERE. I'LL STAY TO HELP WITH IT.
I GUESS THIS IS FINALLY OVER.

THERE IS SOMETHING ELSE OUTSIDE OF MY JURISDICTION. SOMETHING YOU MIGHT BE INTERESTED IN.
LAST WEEK A SHIP LEFT HERE BOUND FOR GOTHAM CITY IN AMERICA...

THE HONG KONG POLICE HAD LOTS OF QUESTIONS.
THE MYSTERIOUS FRENCH GUY DIDN'T STICK AROUND TO ANSWER ANY OF THEM. NEITHER DID I.
PACIFIC JEWEL

BUT HE DID GIVE ME THE NAME OF DORRANCE'S SHIP:
THE PACIFIC JEWEL.

ITS CARGO IS SIR EDMUND'S LEGACY.
THIS IS WHAT ALL OF THIS HAS BEEN ABOUT.

THIS IS WHAT CLYDE RAWLINS DIED FOR.
AND DORRANCE WAS WILLING TO KILL MILLIONS FOR.

THERE'S PROBABLY HUNDREDS OF MILLIONS HERE.
DOLLARS, POUND NOTES, DEUTSCHMARKS AND YEN.

ALL OF IT HAS BLOOD ON IT.
I KNOW. I'VE SEEN THE BLOOD.

IT WAS GOING TO GIVE DORRANCE A NEW START IN GOTHAM.
A NEW WORLD TO CORRUPT.

THAT'S ALL OVER NOW.
IT'S REALLY ALL OVER NOW.
LYNX.

JUST ONE THING LEFT TO DO.
I'VE BEEN WAITING FOR THIS, LYNX...

WHAT...
YOU WANT TO PUNISH ME? GO ON!
OR DON'T YOU WANT TO LOOK AT ME?

LOOK AT ME!
I WAS PUNISHED BECAUSE OF YOU! SCARRED BECAUSE OF YOU!

OH, I WAS BEAUTIFUL ONCE...

YOU'VE BEEN BACK A WEEK AND YOU DIDN'T CALL.
I WANTED TO SEE THIS THROUGH ON MY OWN.

YOU'VE BEEN HERE ALL ALONG?
WHY DIDN'T YOU STEP IN?
YOU. MET AN ACQUAINTANCE OF MINE. HENRI DUCARD. HE LET WORD GET BACK ABOUT THIS SHIP.
YOU DIDN'T NEED ME.
YOU LOOK READY. ARE YOU?
IS YOUR EDUCATION FINISHED?
DO YOU EVER GET TIRED?
DO YOU EVER WONDER IF WHAT WE DO MAKES ANY DIFFERENCE?
IT DOES TO ME.
THAT'S ALL I ASK.
FOR HIM IT ISN'T ABOUT SAVING THE WORLD.
IT'S ABOUT SAVING HIMSELF.
AND WHY AM I HERE?
I DON'T KNOW THE ANSWER TO THAT ONE.
I GUESS MY EDUCATION IS JUST BEGINNING.
THE END

UNUSED ROBIN COSTUME DESIGNS

Design Art by Neal Adams

Design Art by Norm Breyfogle

Design Art by Norm Breyfogle

Design Art by Norm Breyfogle

Design Art by George Peréz

Design Art by Stephen De Stefano and Tom Lyle

Design Art by Norm Breyfogle and Tom Lyle

Design Art by Norm Breyfogle and Tom Lyle

Design Art by Jim Aparo and Tom Lyle

FINAL BATMAN AND ROBIN DESIGN

Batman Design Art by Graham Nolan

Robin Design Art by Neal Adams and Tom Lyle

Robin Poster by Neal Adams

ROBIN™

A HERO REBORN

Robin: A Hero Reborn TPB
Cover by Brian Bolland